Adventures in Grilling

BOOKS BY GEORGE HIRSCH WITH MARIE BIANCO

Grilling with Chef George Hirsch
Gather 'Round the Grill: A Year of Celebrations

Adventures in GRILLING

George Hirsch

with Marie Bianco

Hearst Books / New York

It is the policy of William Morrow and Company, Inc., and its imprints and
affiliates, recognizing the importance of preserving what has been written, to
print the books we publish on acid-free paper, and we exert our best efforts to
that end.

Library of Congress Cataloging-in-Publication Data
Hirsch, George.
    Adventures in grilling / by George P. Hirsch with Marie Bianco.
—1st ed.
        p.   cm.
    Includes index.
    ISBN 0-688-14569-8
    1. Barbecue cookery.   I. Bianco, Marie.   II. Title.
TX840.B3H554   1996a
641.5'784—dc20   95-48300
                                                                                 CIP

Printed in the United States of America

First Edition

1 2 3 4 5 6 7 8 9 10

BOOK DESIGN BY RICHARD ORIOLO

To the memories of Frank Barba,
who instilled the adventure in me,
and to Louis Rotella—
Happy Days

Acknowledgments

When I sign off on the introduction at the beginning of my television show, I always tell the audience, "Don't go away. I'm going to light the grill," and there are many people in my grilling circle who help light that grill.

I would like to extend my thanks and appreciation to the long list of people who help drive this current adventure:

To the family at the grill, Dori and JoAnn;

Always Pauline and George;

To Diane, Celine, Tom, Bob, Val, Tricia, Kevin, Angela, Brian, Michael, Nancy and Tim;

To Mickey;

To Dick, Pete, and all of the Hirsch clan;

And to all those who make the television series and books possible:

To Char-broil, Hickory Specialties, Walt Disney World, and Hearst Books;

To Whitehawk and Dan, Carol, Norm, Steve, Jack and Joel;

To WLIW, Channel 21, Long Island;

To Arlene;

To Frank Bianco;

To Marie Bianco.

And to all my readers and viewers who have written and to all those I have met on the road. I thank you for your many kind words.

When you have fun with family and friends, cooking will always be an ADVENTURE!

Contents

Introduction   1

Know Your Fire   3

Basics   7

Italy   17

France   69

Spain   83

Germany   91

Scandinavia   113

Canada   123

The United Kingdom   137

Mexico, Central and Latin America, and the Caribbean   159

The Middle East   193

Pacific Rim   205

Index   221

INTRODUCTION

Probably the oldest cooking technique, grilling is a part of cuisines all over the world. "The taste of char must have done something unusually stimulating to the dull, primitive palate," writes James Beard in *Delights and Prejudices*, "and the surprise of first smelling smoke and then tasting the food probably created the first step toward 'gourmandism.'"

Whether you're stepping up to the grill for the first time or have smelled the smoke for as long as you can remember, travel with me around the world to experience the different cultures and their cuisines as we do in our latest PBS television series, "International Grilling with George Hirsch." From the shorelines rimming the Pacific Ocean from China and Japan down to Australia, to the vast open spaces and abundant streams of Canada, to the loose and loud streets of Mexico, and everywhere in between, there is plenty of good grilling going on.

Turn to any page in this book and find yourself at kitchen tables (and backyard grills) from around the world. From our neighbors to the north comes Maple-grilled Rutabaga. If you've never visited the British Isles (or even if you have), let each bite of Shepherd's Pie, Irish Stew, or Cock-a-Leekie Soup take you there. One of my favorite grilled foods is pizza—yes, pizza—and it seems I can never prepare enough Imam Flat Bread, pizza with a Middle Eastern personality. If you love Asian food but can't imagine preparing it at home, try my simple-to-prepare Vegetable Spring Rolls, Turkey-and-Black-Bean Wontons, or Japanese Pork Spare Ribs Teriyaki, using ingredients from your local supermarket. Chorizo Stew and Chicken in Garlic Sauce demonstrate just how perfectly the rustic flavors of Spanish cuisine lend themselves to the grill. Of course, there are plenty of recipes that will make you feel as though you're cooking over an open fire in the hills of Tuscany—and everywhere else in Italy. Classic pizzas, pastas, grilled fish, beef, chicken, and veal as well as antipasti can be turned out from the grill.

And whether you're a neophyte in the kitchen or an accomplished cook, you'll love preparing French-inspired Oyster Stew, Seared Duck Breast with Greens and Grilled Fruit, and Lyonnaise Potatoes in your own backyard.

As in my previous books, I have brought out of doors many of the dishes ordinarily prepared in the kitchen. Indeed, I discovered that grilling can be a speedy way to prepare otherwise time-consuming dishes. German foods adapt especially well. My version of Sauerbraten Steak need be marinated only one day rather than three or four. Prepare Spätzle in no time following my simple directions. I've also adapted all of your Mexican favorites to the grill, from Burritos, Empanadas, and Tamales to Posole and Smoked Vegetable Soup.

However far afield you decide to go, savor the sights, smells, sounds, textures, and tastes of these dishes. Choose ingredients with an eye toward color and size. Place them on the grill, stand back and breathe in the mouthwatering aromas, listen to the hiss and sizzle, then savor the flavors.

KNOW YOUR FIRE

I am often asked to reveal my cooking secrets and to explain my grilling techniques. In one phrase, I give away my quintessential secret, the advice I use to close every television show: "Know your fire." It is my cooking credo, one that can play a big part in your everyday cooking. Here's how.

When you instill passion in someone, you fire them up, you bring to life what was dormant and potential. In a very real sense, bringing fire to food does the same thing. Fire gives food another life, another layer of flavor, an identity separate from its prefired past. What's more, bringing the passion you've developed for food to every meal you prepare and eat gives it yet another life.

Ask most chefs who their first major culinary influence was and they will likely give the same answer—Grandma, Nana, or Nona. They will recall their earliest food memories as fondly as world travelers remember their first trip. Whether or not you remember them, food influences began almost from the day you were born. Long before you were tall enough to see what was cooking on the stove or roasting in the oven, the sights, sounds, and surroundings in which food was eaten influenced your relationship with food. You were getting to know your fire.

I grew up in a predominantly Italian and German household where meals generally reflected the cuisines of these two countries. Among my best friends were an Irishman and a Cuban. Whenever I ate with their families, my fire was fueled even more, my food experiences opened to different fragrances, tastes, and textures. From my first taste of horseradish to that first bite into a plantain, my ever-expanding palate was tantalized by the possibilities. Today, you don't have to live in an ethnically diverse neighborhood or have a grandma, nana, or nona in order to add fuel to your fire. Many unusual, exotic ingredients are available in your local supermarket. You'll find tortillas in Minnesota, wild rice in San Antonio, saffron in Wyoming, and Dungeness crabs in Atlanta.

The next time you go to the market, pick up one new food item and take your taste buds on a cultural tour, even if it means trying eggplant for the first time or cooking plantains with a southern twist. You will broaden your fire. In time, if you have stoked that fire and fed it regularly, your family and friends will benefit as you prepare foods that your ancestors enjoyed or are inspired by the places you have visited. I have discovered that I knew my fire all along— long before I lit the stove or the grill. So, read on and begin to explore the fires of other cultures. Consider this my personal invitation to "know your fire," and enjoy this adventure in grilling.

A Few Tips from the Chef

Get a Safe Handle on Your Grillables

- The smaller the piece of meat, seafood, or produce, the faster it loses important vitamins and minerals. Small portions are also more susceptible to bacteria. For example, chopped meat will spoil faster than a roast because its many surfaces are exposed to more air. Fresh poultry is best when used within two days. Ground meat should be cooked within twenty-four hours, or frozen up to one month. I don't like freezing foods for longer than that, with the exception of large roasts.

- During the warmer months, avoid keeping food frozen for long periods. Every time you open and close the freezer door, warm air enters and creates ice crystals.

- The temperature in your refrigerator should be between 35 and 38°F. The produce drawers, on the other hand, should reach 40°F to preserve their moisture. The freezer should be set at 0°F.

- Frozen food should never be left on the kitchen counter to defrost. Not only does it provide the perfect atmosphere for bacteria, but the dramatic temperature drop causes the food to lose moisture. The day before you plan to use it, place the food on the lower shelf of your refrigerator to thaw.

- When cooking meat, take it out of the refrigerator thirty to sixty minutes before cooking so that it reaches room temperature. The cooking times in all of the recipes are based on foods at room temperature.

- When deep-frying, whether on a grill, side burner, or stove, avoid salting the food first because salt can cause the fat to bubble up and possibly rise up over the rim of the pan. Strain the oil often to remove burned particles.

Above all, never deep-fry in high-traffic areas, and keep children and pets away.

- Use a meat thermometer to test for doneness. All meat should reach an internal temperature of 160°F. Keep in mind that the internal heat continues to cook meat, so it is safe to remove meat when it registers five to ten degrees less than its final "done" temperature.

The Ultimate Question: Grill with the Cover Up or Down?

One of the questions I am most frequently asked is, "Do I grill with the cover up or down?" I always respond with the same answer: "It depends." If your grill is functioning properly and reaching the proper temperatures, it will retain heat without any significant temperature loss, and you can leave the grill cover up. This is referred to as "grilling with dry heat," and it's the cooking method used for grilling steak, or any meat, fish, poultry, or produce less than 1 inch thick. Examine your grill to determine whether it is working efficiently.

I grill with the lid up when I want a good browned sear on the outside of whatever I'm grilling. Once the food is browned, I lower the lid. For example, when I grill a whole chicken or a thick piece of meat, I sear it first to seal in the juices, lower the temperature, then I close the cover to cook the chicken or meat thoroughly without charring the outside.

I always consider the weather when it comes to grilling with the lid up or down. On cold days or when it's very windy, keep a closer eye on the grill temperature and close the lid to keep in the heat. A closed hood also results in a smokier flavor.

BASICS

In this chapter you'll find ways to grill many of the ingredients you'll be using throughout this book. Although times and temperatures are listed, they are simply suggestions. Times will vary according to the outside temperature and the thickness of the food. Use the instructions as guidelines. You'll find recipes for chicken stock and fish stock that are easier and less time consuming than standard ones.

You'll also find flavored oils and vinegars to add new dimensions to salads and grilled foods. Brush eggplant slices with the Basil Olive Oil or try marinating mushrooms in your favorite vinaigrette dressing before grilling. Discover how much depth a little Caramelized Garlic gives to olive oil.

Grilled Vegetables

Bell peppers: Cut the peppers from stem to base and separate the halves. Remove the stem ends and attached seeds and cut away the whitish ribs with a paring knife. Brush both sides lightly with olive oil, and grill over high heat for 2 to 3 minutes per side.

Bok choy: Cut stems. Dip leaves in water, drizzle with oil. Quickly grill for 30 seconds over medium heat. Brush stems with oil and cook over medium heat for 1 minute.

Chili peppers: Brush with olive oil and grill over medium-high heat until charred, 2 to 3 minutes per side. Cool slightly, cut in half, and remove seeds.

Corn: Discard the husks and silk, brush with olive oil, and grill over medium-high heat, turning several times, until slightly charred, about 15 to 20 minutes.

Eggplant: Slice thinly lengthwise, brush lightly with olive oil, and grill over medium heat 2 to 3 minutes on each side.

Carmelized garlic: Slice 1/4 inch from the bottom of whole heads of garlic, rub with olive oil, and place on the grill, cut side down, over low heat. After about 20 minutes, cover loosely with foil and cook until carmelized, about 25 to 35 minutes longer.

Ginger: Cut into long thin strips, brush lightly with olive oil, and grill over medium-high heat until lightly browned, about 2 minutes on each side.

Leeks: Cut off and discard the root base and green stalks. Separate the leaves and wash well under cool running water. Drain, brush with olive oil, and grill over medium-high heat until tender, about 5 minutes, turning frequently.

Mushrooms: Rinse quickly under cool water to remove dirt and pat dry. Brush with olive oil and grill over medium-high heat for 4 to 5 minutes for small mushrooms. For larger mushrooms, such as Portobellos, continue cooking at cooler grill edges until tender, 6 to 8 minutes longer.

Onions: Cut horizontally into 1/2- to 3/4-inch slices, brush lightly with olive oil, and grill over high heat until tender, 3 to 4 minutes per side.

Plum tomatoes: Cut in half through the stem ends. Brush with olive oil and grill over high heat, cut sides down, until lightly charred, about 2 to 3 minutes per side.

Potatoes: Wash whole potatoes and pat dry. Rub with vegetable oil, wrap individually in aluminum foil, and grill over medium-high heat for 35 to 40 minutes. A potato is done when a paring knife inserts easily in the center.

Radicchio: Cut in half. Sprinkle on all sides with 2 tablespoons olive oil and 4 tablespoons chicken stock. Grill over medium heat for 2 minutes on each side.

Scallions: Cut off the stem ends and brush lightly with olive oil. Grill over high heat for 4 to 5 minutes, turning several times.

Shallots: Cut off the stem ends, brush with olive oil, and grill for 10 minutes over low heat. Cover with aluminum foil and grill for 4 to 5 minutes longer.

Zucchini and yellow squash: Wash, dry, and slice 1/4 inch thick. Brush with olive oil and grill for 2 minutes per side over medium heat.

Grilled Fruits

Apples: Core the apples, peel if desired, and cut in half or crosswise into thick slices. Brush with melted butter and grill over medium heat until lightly charred, 4 to 5 minutes per side.

Pineapple: Peel and remove top. Cut horizontally into $1/2$-inch slices, lightly brush with melted butter, and grill on medium-high heat for 4 to 5 minutes per side.

Toasted Nuts

Melt 1 tablespoon of butter in a small skillet, add 1 cup of chopped nuts or seeds, and cook over low heat, shaking the pan frequently, until they turn light brown, about 5 minutes.

Grilled Meats

Ham steaks: Brush lightly with olive oil and grill on both sides over medium heat for 4 to 5 minutes total.

Sausage: Split in half lengthwise. Grill flat sides down 4 to 5 minutes over medium heat.

Chicken Stock

4 pounds chicken bones (necks, backs, etc.)

2 onions, quartered

2 carrots, cut into large chunks

2 ribs celery, cut into large chunks

1 each: white turnip, leek, parsnip (optional)

4 cloves garlic

6 black peppercorns

2 bay leaves

3 parsley stems

1 whole clove

Pinch dried thyme

GRILL TEMPERATURE
high, then low

Makes
8 cups

Preheat the grill or side burner.

Wash the chicken bones in cool running water and place them in a large kettle. Add the onion, carrot, celery, and turnip, leek, and parsnip, if using. Add the garlic, peppercorns, bay leaves, parsley stems, clove, and thyme. Add 10 cups of cold water, bring to a boil, reduce the heat, and simmer for 1½ hours. Skim the surface several times with a ladle to remove any scum. Strain the stock, discarding all the vegetables, and chill as quickly as possible. The stock can be refrigerated up to 2 days or frozen up to 1 month.

Fish Stock

2 pounds fish bones (cod, halibut, bass, shellfish, etc.)

2 tablespoons butter

1½ onions, peeled and quartered

2 ribs celery, cut into large chunks

1 leek, cleaned, white part only

3 cloves garlic

1 cup dry white wine

3 cloves garlic

3 parsley stems

4 black peppercorns

1 clove

Pinch dried thyme

Preheat the grill or side burner.

Wash the fish bones under cool running water. Heat the butter in a soup kettle, add the onion, celery, leek, and garlic, and sauté for 5 minutes. Add the fish bones, 6 cups of cold water, wine, garlic, parsley, peppercorns, clove, and thyme. Bring the mixture to a boil, lower the heat, and simmer for 35 minutes. Skim the surface of any scum during cooking. Strain the stock, discard the solids, and chill immediately. The stock can be refrigerated for 48 hours or frozen for 1 month.

Caramelized Garlic Olive Oil

1 head Caramelized Garlic (page 8)
Freshly ground black pepper to taste
³/₄ cup virgin olive oil

Makes
almost
1 cup

Puree half the garlic cloves. Add the pureed garlic, whole garlic cloves, and black pepper to the oil and pour into a sterile dark glass bottle with a tight-fitting cap. The oil can be used after 1 hour, but the flavor improves overnight. Do not store in the refrigerator.

Hot Pepper Oil

2 tablespoons olive oil
2 serrano chilies, or ¹/₂ habanero or Scotch bonnet chili
1 cup virgin olive oil

Makes
1 cup

Heat the 2 tablespoons of olive oil in a small saucepan. Add the chilies and cook slowly over low heat to draw out the heat from the chilies, about 10 minutes. Cool the oil and chilies and combine with the 1 cup olive oil. Store in a sterile dark glass bottle with a tight-fitting cap. The oil can be used after 1 hour, but the flavor improves after a day. Do not store in the refrigerator.

Basil Olive Oil

¹/₄ cup fresh basil leaves, washed and patted completely dry

Freshly ground black pepper to taste

³/₄ cup virgin olive oil

Puree half the basil in a blender or food processor. Combine the pureed basil, the whole basil leaves, and pepper with the olive oil. Store in a sterile dark glass bottle with a tight-fitting cap. The oil can be used in 1 hour, but the flavor improves after a day. Do not store in the refrigerator.

Lemon Olive Oil

Peel from 2 lemons

Zest of 1 lemon

Freshly ground black pepper to taste

1 cup virgin olive oil

Preheat the grill.

Sear the lemon peel on the grill until crisp but not black. Remove and cool. Add the lemon peel, lemon zest, and pepper to the olive oil and store in a sterile dark glass jar with a tight-fitting cap. The oil can be used after 1 hour, but the flavor improves overnight. Do not store in the refrigerator.

Herb Vinegar

1 cup cider vinegar

1 stem fresh rosemary

2 sprigs fresh thyme

2 sprigs fresh parsley

1 teaspoon crushed black peppercorns

1 jalapeño or serrano pepper

Makes
1 cup

Combine all of the ingredients and store in a sterile dark glass jar with a tight-fitting cap. The vinegar can be used after 2 to 3 days.

Vinaigrette Dressing

$1/4$ cup olive oil

2 tablespoons balsamic vinegar

1 green olive, chopped

2 cloves Caramelized Garlic (page 8), pureed

1 teaspoon dried thyme

$1/2$ teaspoon Tabasco

Makes about
$1/2$ cup

Combine all of the ingredients and mix well.

ITALY

Grilling has a long history in Italy. In Venice, fish harvested fresh from the Adriatic is grilled over a hot fire and dressed with a squirt of lemon juice and a drizzle of fruity olive oil. Classic Tuscan beefsteak is seasoned with only pepper and top-quality Tuscan olive oil. It doesn't get much simpler or more flavorful than that. Italians begin dinner with antipasti which, literally translated, means "before the pasta." We've included both hot and cold antipasti with enough selections to fashion a whole meal around these tasty tidbits. And, of course, there are pasta dishes galore. Cooked on the grill? Sure. Prepare the sauce on the grill while the water boils on a side burner.

The hills outside Rome are blanketed with wooly sheep and suckling lamb, the famous abbacchio. We'll show you at least a half dozen ways to make you feel as though you're cooking over an open fire in the hills of Tuscany. And the Italians do not ignore chicken, so either have we, including the traditional Chicken Cacciatore to the popular Chicken Scarpariello.

Before the food goes on the grill, throw a few bay leaves onto the fire or vine cuttings that have been soaked in water for 20 minutes. The aromas will heighten the flavor of the food, as well as your appetite.

Hot Smoked Pork Tenderloin

I prefer serving antipasto in courses, first cold and then hot. A selection of hot antipasti is just as colorful and flavorful as a cold one and can make a complete buffet just by itself.

Three 10- to 12-ounce pork tenderloins
¹/₂ cup Pork Smoke Rub (page 20)
Wood chips (oak or fruitwood)

Trim all fat from the tenderloins and remove the silver skin. Rub the meat with the Pork Smoke Rub, cover well, and refrigerate for 24 hours.

Preheat the grill.

Soak the wood chips in water for 30 minutes. Place them in an iron smoker box or aluminum-foil pan and place inside the grill. Close the cover and let the wood smolder for 4 to 5 minutes.

Place the pork on the grill and cook for 12 to 15 minutes with the grill cover down, turning occasionally, or until the meat is cooked (160°F on a meat thermometer). Remove the meat and let it rest for 5 minutes before slicing.

GRILL TEMPERATURE
medium-low

Makes
8 servings

Italy

Pork Smoke Rub

**Makes almost
3 tablespoons**

1 teaspoon sweet paprika

1 teaspoon ground cumin

1 teaspoon ground coriander

1 teaspoon black pepper

1 teaspoon garlic powder

1 teaspoon dried parsley

1 teaspoon dried oregano

1 teaspoon dried thyme

Combine all of the ingredients in a small bowl and mix well. Store in a tightly covered container.

Pork Medallions with Melon

If you like prosciutto and melon, you'll like this combination. The peppery pork offsets the richness of the wine-soaked melon.

One 12-ounce pork tenderloin

¼ cup prepared mustard

½ teaspoon dried rosemary, crushed

3 tablespoons crushed peppercorns

1 cantaloupe, seeded and sliced

½ cup red wine

Preheat the grill.

Cut the pork tenderloin into ½-inch slices, brush with the mustard. Coat with the rosemary and peppercorns. Grill the pork for 3 to 4 minutes on each side; remove and chill. Sear the melon for 2 minutes on each side. Remove and set in a shallow dish with the wine. Marinate, refrigerated, for 1 hour. Serve the pork medallions with the melon and red-wine juices.

GRILL TEMPERATURE
high

Makes
8 appetizer
servings

Italy

Eggplant and Cheese Fingers

GRILL TEMPERATURE

medium-high for eggplant; high for cheese

Makes 4 servings

Children love to eat finger foods. Eggplant may not be one of their favorite foods, but if it's cut into finger-size pieces, grilled, and dipped in a sauce, kids might be tempted to at least try one. Of course, adults will love these, too.

¹/₂ cup all-purpose flour

1 teaspoon crushed black peppercorns

Pinch ground nutmeg

1 small eggplant, peeled and cut into finger-size pieces

8 ounces mozzarella cheese, cut into finger-size pieces

¹/₄ cup olive oil

1 cup Caramelized Garlic and Tomato Dip (recipe follows)

Preheat the grill or side burner.

Combine the flour, pepper, and nutmeg in a shallow bowl. Dip the eggplant and cheese fingers in the mixture and shake off any excess. Heat the olive oil in a sauté pan until very hot. Quickly cook the eggplant until light brown on all sides. Remove and drain on paper towels. Cook the mozzarella fingers quickly on a hot grill for 30 seconds so that the outsides brown but the cheese does not melt. Serve with the Caramelized Garlic and Tomato Dip.

Caramelized Garlic and Tomato Dip

Sticky, sweet caramelized garlic balances perfectly the acidic tomato. Serve toasted pita triangles with this dip.

Makes about 2 cups

> 12 plum tomatoes, grilled (page 9) and chopped
>
> 2 heads Caramelized Garlic (page 8), pureed
>
> ½ onion, sliced, grilled (page 9), and chopped
>
> 4 leaves fresh basil, coarsely chopped
>
> ½ cup mascarpone cheese, at room temperature

In a medium saucepan, combine the tomato, garlic, onion, and basil and simmer for 5 minutes. Stir in the mascarpone and cook until the dip is warm.

Italy

Calamari and Red Onion Salad

GRILL
TEMPERATURE
high

**Makes 8
appetizer
servings**

Calamari is served in trattorias all over Italy. It suffers from a reputation for being tough and chewy, but that's because it is often overcooked. Cooked until just opaque, it is tender and succulent.

1 pound calamari, cleaned and sliced into ¼-inch rings

1 red onion, sliced thin, grilled (page 9) until light brown

3 tablespoons olive oil

1 tablespoon balsamic vinegar

2 teaspoons fennel seeds

Preheat the grill.

Sear the calamari rings and remove them as soon as they become opaque. Take care not to overcook them or they will become rubbery. Mix the calamari with the onion, olive oil, vinegar, and fennel seeds, and refrigerate for 1 hour before serving.

Grilled Radicchio and Hot Pepper Salad

GRILL
TEMPERATURE
medium

Makes
6 servings

Also known as Italian chicory, radicchio can be tossed into salads raw or grilled as I do here. If you're watching your fat intake, grill the peppers for 4 to 5 minutes instead of frying them.

2 pounds Italian hot peppers

1 cup vegetable oil for frying

2 serrano chilies

6 cloves Caramelized Garlic (page 8), pureed

2 heads radicchio, cut into eight pieces total and grilled (page 9)

1 tablespoon balsamic vinegar

1 tablespoon extra-virgin Italian olive oil

1 tablespoon coarsely chopped fresh Italian parsley

Freshly ground black pepper to taste

Preheat the grill or side burner.

Heat the oil in a heavy skillet to 325°F. Fry the peppers on all sides, turning them occasionally, until the skins begin to blister, 2 to 3 minutes. Remove the peppers and drain them on paper towels. When the peppers are cool enough to handle, split them vertically and discard the seeds. Arrange the peppers on a serving dish with the caramelized garlic and grilled radicchio. Drizzle with the balsamic vinegar and olive oil; garnish with the parsley and a grinding of black pepper.

Olive and Arugula Salad

While extremely popular in Italy, arugula is still finding its way onto America's dinner plates. When it is fresh and at its peak, I can't pass it up, so I'm always searching for different ways to prepare it. This simple preparation is a favorite.

4 cups arugula (about 2 bunches)

½ cup pitted Niçoise olives, coarsely chopped

½ head Caramelized Garlic (page 8), pureed

2 teaspoons dry mustard

Freshly ground black pepper to taste

Juice and zest of 1 lemon

4 tablespoons olive oil

2 tablespoons shaved Parmesan cheese, or 1 tablespoon grated

Wash the arugula well and remove any sand. Trim the stems, if desired.

Crush half the olives and mix with the garlic, mustard, and pepper. Stir in the lemon juice and zest and whip in the olive oil. Stir in the remaining olives. Pour the dressing over the arugula, toss lightly, and top with freshly ground pepper and the shaved Parmesan cheese.

Bruschetta with a Trio of Cheeses

My Uncle Dick became a great home chef after his early retirement. In true Italian fashion, he would make this *bruschetta* first and then eat it while he cooked the rest of the meal.

GRILL
TEMPERATURE
medium

Makes
6 to 8 servings

1 thin loaf French bread or 1 baguette

4 tablespoons olive oil

1 head Caramelized Garlic (page 8), pureed

1 cup ricotta cheese, well drained

¼ cup Gorgonzola cheese

¼ cup grated Parmesan cheese

4 fresh basil leaves, coarsely chopped

Freshly ground black pepper to taste

Preheat the grill.

Cut the bread into ½-inch slices on an angle, brush with the olive oil, and spread with the garlic puree. Lightly toast the bread on both sides on the grill.

Combine the ricotta, Gorgonzola, Parmesan, basil, and pepper in a small bowl and spread liberally on the bread. Serve immediately.

Italy

Crostini

Literally "little toasts" in Italian, *crostini* are the smaller more delicate first cousins to *bruschetta*, the original garlic bread.

**Makes
6 servings**

12 slices Italian bread

3 tablespoons olive oil

12 cloves Caramelized Garlic (page 8), pureed

6 mushrooms, grilled (page 9) and chopped

1 red bell pepper, grilled (page 8) and cut into 1-inch strips

Parmesan cheese shavings

Freshly ground black pepper to taste

Preheat the grill.

Lightly brush the bread with half the olive oil, and grill. Grill for 30 seconds on each side. Watch the slices carefully so they do not burn. Remove the bread from the grill and spread evenly with the caramelized garlic. Top the *crostini* with the mushrooms, red-pepper strips, Parmesan, and black pepper. Return the *crostini* to the grill and heat for 1 minute. Serve with soup.

Pizza Toasts

Whenever I visit La Mela in Little Italy, Mimmo and Pepe always have their version of *bruschetta*, ready and waiting. Welcome your next guests with some pizza toasts hot off the grill.

GRILL TEMPERATURE
medium

**Makes
4 servings**

> **1 loaf day-old Tuscan-style bread, sliced 1 inch thick**
>
> **¼ cup olive oil**
>
> **1 cup pizza sauce (commercial or homemade)**
>
> **½ cup shredded mozzarella cheese**
>
> **2 tablespoons grated Parmesan cheese**
>
> **½ teaspoon dried oregano**

Preheat the grill.

Brush the bread with the olive oil and quickly toast on both sides on the grill. Top one side with the pizza sauce, mozzarella, and Parmesan cheese and return to the grill until the cheese melts. Sprinkle with a pinch of oregano and serve immediately.

Italy

Panzanella
(Tuscan Bread Salad)

Panzanella, once considered a poor man's salad in Rome and Tuscany, is made from stale bread. I prefer to describe it as a smart man's salad because it's a creative way to avoid wasting bread.

1 loaf two-day-old Tuscan bread, sliced 1 inch thick

1 head Caramelized Garlic (page 8), pureed

¼ cup olive oil

1 red onion, sliced and grilled (page 9)

1 red bell pepper, grilled (page 8) and chopped

**1 small zucchini or yellow squash, split lengthwise, grilled (page 9),
   and chopped**

½ cup mushrooms, grilled (page 9) and sliced

½ cup Tomato-Basil Dressing (recipe follows)

4 fresh basil leaves, coarsely chopped

1 tablespoon chopped fresh sage

Preheat the grill.

Rub the sliced bread on both sides with the garlic and brush with olive oil. Cut the bread into 1-inch crouton-size pieces and toast on the grill. Place the bread in a bowl and add the onion, red pepper, zucchini, and mushrooms. Pour the Tomato-Basil Dressing over the ingredients and toss well. Garnish with the chopped basil and sage.

Tomato-Basil Dressing

8 plum tomatoes, grilled (page 9) and chopped

2 tablespoons coarsely chopped fresh basil

1 tablespoon olive oil

1 tablespoon balsamic vinegar

1 teaspoon dry mustard

$1/2$ teaspoon Tabasco

Freshly ground black pepper to taste

Makes
1 cup

Combine all of the ingredients and set aside for 1 hour to let the flavors blend.

Italy

Minestrone

GRILL
TEMPERATURE

**medium, then
low**

Makes
6 servings

As with all soups, this one tastes much better when it's made a day in advance. Add the cooked pasta just before you serve it so that it doesn't become soggy. Add extra pasta to make a hearty vegetarian entree, or serve with *crostini* for a satisfying lunch.

2 tablespoons olive oil

1/2 onion, sliced, grilled (page 9), and chopped

1 green bell pepper, grilled (page 8) and chopped

1 red bell pepper, grilled (page 8) and chopped

1/4 cup diced carrot

1/4 cup diced celery

1 head Caramelized Garlic (page 8), pureed

2 to 3 plum tomatoes, grilled (page 9) and chopped

1/2 cup tomato puree

6 cups Chicken Stock (page 11) or vegetable stock

3 bay leaves

1/2 teaspoon dried oregano

1/2 teaspoon dried basil

1/2 teaspoon Tabasco

1/2 cup 1-inch-cut green beans

1/2 cup dry white beans, such as Great Northern or cannellini, cooked, or 1 cup canned white beans

1 cup cooked small pasta such as ditalini, orzo, elbows, or shells

Preheat the grill or side burner.

Heat the oil in a large stockpot or soup kettle. Add the onion, green and red peppers, carrot, celery, and garlic and sauté for 2 minutes. Stir in the tomato and tomato puree and cook for 4 to 5 minutes. Add the stock, bring to a boil, and reduce the heat to a simmer. Add the bay leaves, oregano, basil, and Tabasco. Simmer for 45 minutes; add the green beans and cook for 15 to 20 minutes longer. Stir in the cooked beans and pasta and simmer until they're heated through. Discard the bay leaves before serving.

Chicken and Garlic Soup

During my television series, I often refer to Norm, who is my cameraman and number-one critic. Norm loves garlic and this is a favorite of his.

**Makes
6 servings**

One 2¹/₂-pound chicken, cut into 10 pieces

4 tablespoons olive oil

1 cup chopped tomato

1 large onion, grilled (page 9) and chopped

¹/₂ cup chopped celery

1 leek, cleaned, white part only, chopped

3 heads Caramelized Garlic (page 8), pureed

6 cups Chicken Stock (page 11)

2 cups day-old French bread, grilled and cut into croutons

2 bay leaves

¹/₂ teaspoon Tabasco

¹/₄ cup green olives, pitted and coarsely chopped

Preheat the grill.

Brush both sides of the chicken with 2 tablespoons of olive oil and sear on a hot grill for 1 minute on each side.

Preheat the side burner.

In a 4-quart stockpot, heat the remaining 2 tablespoons of olive oil and cook the tomato, onion, celery, leek, and garlic for 2 minutes. Add the stock, 1¹/₂ cups of the croutons, bay leaves, and Tabasco. Add the chicken pieces, and bring to a boil, lower the heat, and simmer for 15 to 20 minutes. Add the olives and simmer for 15 minutes. Discard the bay leaves. Ladle the soup into bowls and top with the remaining croutons.

Farfalle Alfredo

GRILL
TEMPERATURE
medium

Makes
4 servings

Farfalle are pasta shaped like butterflies or bow ties. Farfallini are smaller in size; farfalloni are much bigger. *Alfredo* refers to Alfredo di Lello, a Roman restaurateur who created fettuccine Alfredo more than sixty years ago.

1 tablespoon olive oil

1 tablespoon butter

1/2 onion, sliced, grilled (page 9), and chopped

6 cloves Caramelized Garlic (page 8), pureed

1 pound farfalle (bow-tie pasta), cooked

2 cups heavy cream or half-and-half

1/2 cup grated Parmesan cheese

2 tablespoons chopped fresh basil

Pinch ground nutmeg

Freshly ground black pepper to taste

Preheat the grill or side burner.

Heat the olive oil and butter in a large skillet or saucepan. Add the onion and garlic and sauté for 1 minute. Add the cooked pasta and mix well. Add the cream, Parmesan, basil, nutmeg, and pepper and cook for 2 minutes.

Variations:

• Add 3 to 4 grilled plum tomatoes, chopped, and 1 ounce vodka to the sauce.
• Top the pasta with grilled shrimp.
• Add 2 cups chopped fresh spinach to the sauce.
• Add 1/4 cup crumbled Gorgonzola cheese, 2 ounces hazelnut liqueur, and 2 tablespoons of chopped toasted hazelnuts after the sauce is cooked.

Italy

Fettuccine with Scallops, Shrimp, and Radicchio

GRILL
TEMPERATURE
high, then
medium

Makes
4 servings

Most of the fettuccine in this country is wider than that found in Rome. My Roman cousins always begin Sunday dinner with a plate of fettuccine. The only way this dish could be improved would be by eating it at Mauro and Anna's house.

2 heads radicchio

6 tablespoons olive oil

1½ pounds fettuccine

½ pound bay scallops

1 pound large shrimp, peeled and deveined

¼ cup Seafood Rub (page 38)

1 head Caramelized Garlic (page 8), pureed

2 tablespoons butter

½ cup white wine

Juice of 2 lemons

Freshly ground black pepper to taste

Preheat the grill.

Soak the radicchio in water, remove, shake off the water, and drizzle with 2 tablespoons of olive oil. Sear the radicchio for 2 minutes on a hot grill, turning once. Remove and coarsely chop.

Cook the fettuccine until al dente, drain, toss with 2 tablespoons of olive oil in a large serving bowl, and keep warm.

Toss the scallops and the shrimp with 2 tablespoons of olive oil and sprinkle with half the seasoning mix. Place the seafood on a medium grill and cook for a total of 4 to 5 minutes, turning once. Do not overcook.

While the seafood is cooking, heat the garlic and butter in a saucepan. Add the white wine, lemon juice, and the remaining seasoning mix and bring to a boil. Add the grilled seafood and simmer for 1 minute. Pour the sauce and the grilled radicchio over the fettuccine and toss gently. Sprinkle with black pepper and serve.

Seafood Rub

1 tablespoon chopped fresh basil

1 tablespoon chopped fresh thyme

1 tablespoon chopped fresh Italian parsley

1 teaspoon red pepper flakes, or to taste

1 teaspoon dried oregano

Combine all of the ingredients in a small bowl and mix well. Use immediately.

Spaghetti Carbonara

This lower-fat version of spaghetti carbonara replaces heavy cream and eggs with chicken stock. To make the more traditional dish, substitute 2 cups of heavy cream and 3 egg yolks for the chicken stock. When adding the egg yolk, do not boil the mixture or the eggs will curdle.

GRILL TEMPERATURE
medium

**Makes
4 servings**

4 tablespoons olive oil

**¹/₂ pound ham steak, grilled (page 10) and chopped, or 4 ounces
  sliced prosciutto**

1 onion, grilled (page 9) and chopped

4 cloves Caramelized Garlic (page 8), pureed

1 pound spaghetti, cooked

1 cup Chicken Stock (page 11)

¹/₄ cup grated Parmesan cheese

2 tablespoons butter

1 tablespoon coarsely ground black pepper

Preheat the grill or side burner.

Heat the olive oil in a large skillet and sauté the ham, onion, and garlic for 2 minutes. Add the cooked spaghetti, chicken stock, and Parmesan cheese and toss well. Add the butter, sprinkle with pepper, and serve.

Italy

Risotto with Mushrooms

Arborio rice is traditionally used in risotto because it produces a creamy texture. It's always difficult to give an exact cooking time for risotto because it depends on how quickly the rice absorbs the liquid. The time can be as little as 18 minutes or as much as 25.

Risotto can be made with any number of ingredients, including saffron, prosciutto, shellfish, and spinach.

2 tablespoons olive oil

1 cup sliced mushrooms (shiitake, Portobello, or button), grilled (page 9)

1 onion, sliced, grilled (page 9), and chopped

1 carrot, finely chopped

6 cloves Caramelized Garlic (page 8), pureed

2 cups arborio rice

1/2 cup white wine

1 teaspoon chopped fresh sage

Pinch ground nutmeg

Freshly ground black pepper to taste

4 1/2 to 5 cups hot Chicken Stock (page 11)

Grated Parmesan cheese

Preheat the grill.

Heat the olive oil in a saucepan. Add the mushrooms, onion, carrot, and garlic and cook for 5 minutes over medium-low heat. Add the rice and wine and cook for 2 minutes over low heat. Stir in the sage, nutmeg, and pepper. Add ¼ cup of hot chicken stock and stir constantly until the rice absorbs the liquid. Continue adding the stock, ¼ cup at a time, until the rice is al dente. Just before the rice is cooked, stir in 3 tablespoons of Parmesan cheese. Serve with additional black pepper and Parmesan.

Spaghetti with Wild Mushrooms and Cheese

GRILL
TEMPERATURE
high

**Makes
4 servings**

Never be shy when it comes to seasoning pasta. Think of it as a blank canvas on which you can paint a masterpiece.

1 cup wild mushrooms (Portobello, shiitake, crimini, etc.), sliced

4 tablespoons olive oil

1 head Caramelized Garlic (page 8), pureed

1/4 cup grated Parmesan cheese

1/4 cup crumbled Gorgonzola or blue cheese

1/4 cup green olives, pitted and chopped

6 leaves fresh basil, finely chopped

2 tablespoons coarsely chopped walnuts

Freshly ground black pepper to taste

1 1/2 pounds spaghetti, cooked

Preheat the grill.

Brush the mushrooms with 2 tablespoons of olive oil and sear on a hot grill for 2 minutes. Turn the mushrooms and grill until lightly browned. Transfer the mushrooms to a large serving bowl and add the remaining olive oil, garlic, Parmesan and Gorgonzola cheeses, olives, basil, walnuts, and pepper and toss lightly. Add the spaghetti, toss, and marinate at room temperature for at least 30 minutes before serving.

Barbecued Meatballs

GRILL
TEMPERATURE
high, then low

Makes
4 servings

Combining ground beef with veal and pork gives these meatballs a more complex flavor than when just beef is used. Many supermarkets sell this ground-meat combination for meat loaf.

1 cup bread crumbs from day-old Italian bread

2 tablespoons milk

1 pound ground meat (a combination of beef, pork, and veal)

1/2 onion, sliced, grilled (page 9), and chopped

8 cloves Caramelized Garlic (page 8), pureed

1/4 cup grated Parmesan cheese

1 egg

1 tablespoon chopped fresh Italian parsley

1 teaspoon dried oregano

2 tablespoons olive oil

2 cups tomato sauce (commercial or homemade)

In a medium bowl, combine the bread and milk and set aside for 5 minutes. Add the ground meat, onion, garlic, Parmesan cheese, egg, parsley, and oregano and mix lightly. Shape the mixture into 2-inch balls and chill for 1 hour in the refrigerator.

Preheat the grill.

Brush the meatballs with the olive oil and sear on a hot grill for 4 to 5 minutes, turning on all sides. Heat the tomato sauce in a medium saucepan, add the meatballs, and simmer for at least 10 minutes.

Italy

Beef Steak Pizzaiola

GRILL
TEMPERATURE

**medium-high,
then low**

**Makes
4 servings**

Grilling steaks usually calls for an expensive cut such as a fillet, sirloin, or rib. When you prepare a cheaper cut of beef *pizzaiola* style, the result is fork-tender with a buttery texture.

Four 8-ounce rump or round steaks

4 tablespoons olive oil

1 head Caramelized Garlic (page 8), pureed

Freshly ground black pepper to taste

8 plum tomatoes, grilled (page 9) and chopped

2 cups tomato sauce (commercial or homemade)

$^1\!/_2$ cup white wine

2 tablespoons chopped fresh basil

Preheat the grill.

Brush the steaks with 2 tablespoons of olive oil. Spread half of the garlic on both sides of the steaks and season with the pepper. Sear the steaks for 3 to 4 minutes on each side.

In a saucepan, combine the tomatoes, tomato sauce, remaining garlic, wine, and basil. Add the steaks and simmer for 20 to 30 minutes on the grill or side burner.

Steak with Tomatoes and Olives

This recipe is a quick and easy way to use chuck steak, one of the best steak values around. Leave the fat on while the meat is grilled, then cut it off before serving. Chuck steak is one of the most flavorful cuts, and the self-basting fat makes it ideal for the grill.

GRILL TEMPERATURE
high, then low

**Makes
4 servings**

3 pounds seven-bone (chuck) or blade steak

4 tablespoons olive oil

10 plum tomatoes, grilled (page 9) and chopped

1 head Caramelized Garlic (page 8), pureed

¼ cup black oil-cured olives, pitted

1 tablespoon coarsely chopped fresh basil

Freshly ground black pepper to taste

Preheat the grill.

Rub the steaks with the olive oil, and grill for 3 to 4 minutes on each side. Remove the steaks and place them in a large skillet with the tomatoes, garlic, olives, basil, and pepper. Bring to a boil, lower the heat, and simmer for 2 minutes.

T-bone Steak Florentine Style

GRILL
TEMPERATURE
medium-high

**Makes
2 servings**

It's easy to identify a T-bone steak because the bone is actually shaped like a T and separates the sirloin from the smaller piece of tenderloin.

One 2-pound T-bone steak

1 tablespoon crushed black peppercorns

2 tablespoons olive oil

Preheat the grill.

Rub both sides of the steak with the crushed peppercorns and place on the grill. When the beef is well browned, about 4 to 5 minutes, turn and cook 4 to 5 minutes longer, or until desired doneness is attained. Drizzle with olive oil and serve.

Abbachio of Lamb

Abbachio is Roman dialect for lamb that has been fed only on its mother's milk. This probably the oldest and most traditional way the Italians cook lamb. Serve it over rice or risotto.

GRILL
TEMPERATURE
medium-high

Makes
6 servings

2 pounds lamb shoulder or lamb stew meat

4 slices bacon, chopped

2 tablespoons olive oil

1 onion, sliced and grilled (page 9)

1 head Caramelized Garlic (page 8), pureed

2 tablespoons all-purpose flour

¹/₂ cup balsamic vinegar

2 cups Chicken Stock (page 11)

2 bay leaves

1 teaspoon dried rosemary leaves

Freshly ground black pepper to taste

Preheat the grill.

Place the lamb on the hot grill and brown well on all sides. Cook the bacon in a medium saucepan until it renders its fat. Stir in the olive oil, onion, garlic, and flour and cook over low heat for 2 minutes. Add the browned lamb and vinegar and simmer for 2 minutes. Add the chicken stock, bay leaves, rosemary, and pepper and simmer until the lamb is tender, 45 to 60 minutes. Remove the bay leaves before serving.

Italy

Veal Braciolette

GRILL
TEMPERATURE
**high, then
medium-high**

**Makes
4 servings**

This rolled veal dish features a classic Italian filling of pine nuts, raisins, and cheese. Thin slices of prosciutto can be substituted for the smoked ham steak.

¼ cup bread cubes from day-old Italian bread

2 tablespoons milk

2 tablespoons pine nuts or chopped walnuts

2 tablespoons raisins

2 tablespoons grated Parmesan cheese

1 teaspoon chopped fresh sage

Eight 3-ounce veal scallops, pounded thin

Freshly ground black pepper to taste

½ pound smoked sliced ham steak, grilled (page 10) and chopped

4 tablespoons olive oil

½ cup dry white wine

Zest of 1 lemon

Juice of 2 lemons

¼ cup sliced black olives

In a small bowl, combine the bread, milk, pine nuts, raisins, Parmesan cheese, and sage to make the stuffing.

Preheat the grill.

Lay the veal scallops on a flat surface and sprinkle with pepper. Top equally with the ham. Spread the stuffing evenly over the ham and roll up the veal, starting from the bottom. Secure each roll with a toothpick. Brush the veal with 2 tablespoons of olive oil and sear on a hot grill for 2 minutes on each side.

In a large sauté pan, heat the remaining 2 tablespoons of olive oil, the wine, lemon zest, and juice. Add the veal and olives and simmer for 2 minutes. Remove the toothpicks before serving.

Veal and Grilled Peppers

To get out of the sausage-and-peppers rut, try grilled peppers with veal. Use whatever bell peppers look fresh at the supermarket—I like to use a variety.

**Makes
4 servings**

2 pounds veal stew meat, cut into 2-inch pieces

5 tablespoons olive oil

2 onions, sliced, grilled (page 9), and chopped

1 head Caramelized Garlic (page 8), pureed

Red pepper flakes, to taste

2 cups tomato sauce (commercial or homemade)

6 plum tomatoes, grilled (page 9) and chopped

2 tablespoons balsamic vinegar

1 tablespoon chopped fresh thyme

4 bell peppers (red or green), halved and seeded

Preheat the grill.

Brush the veal with 2 tablespoons of the olive oil. Sear on a hot grill until the meat is well browned on all sides, 4 to 5 minutes.

Heat 1 tablespoon of olive oil in a large saucepan and sauté the onion, garlic, and hot pepper flakes for 2 minutes. Add the browned meat, tomato sauce, tomatoes, vinegar, and thyme and stir well. Bring to a boil, lower the heat, cover, and simmer until the veal is tender, 35 to 40 minutes.

While the stew is cooking, brush the bell peppers with the remaining 2 tablespoons of olive oil and grill over medium heat for 5 minutes, turning frequently. Cut up the peppers and serve with the veal.

Veal Marsala

Veal is very low in fat, so be careful not to overcook it or it will be tough and rubbery. Marsala is a fortified wine with a rich smoky flavor that comes both dry and sweet. Use dry Marsala for savory dishes like this one, and save the sweet Marsala for desserts like zabaglione.

GRILL TEMPERATURE
medium-high

**Makes
4 servings**

1 cup dry Marsala

¹/₂ cup sliced mushrooms

4 tablespoons olive oil

¹/₂ onion, sliced, grilled (page 9), and diced

6 cloves Caramelized Garlic (page 8), pureed

1 tablespoon chopped fresh rosemary

¹/₂ teaspoon Tabasco

4 veal chops

Combine the marsala, mushrooms, olive oil, onion, garlic, rosemary, and Tabasco in a shallow dish and mix well. Place the veal chops in the marinade and refrigerate for 1 hour, turning the chops occasionally.

Preheat the grill.

Grill the chops for 4 to 5 minutes on each side, turning once, or until the desired doneness is attained. Boil the remaining marinade until it reduces slightly. Use it to baste the chops and serve it as a sauce.

Italy

Veal Saltimbocca

GRILL
TEMPERATURE
high, then
medium-high

Makes
4 servings

The best saltimbocca I ever had was served at my aunt's home in Rome. She offered me a second helping but, with my limited Italian, I didn't understand her and just smiled. She spoke a few words to me, I continued to smile, and the entire platter wound up on my plate. I had to be polite, but I didn't eat for two days after that.

2 pounds veal, sliced into approximately sixteen 2-ounce pieces, pounded thin

Freshly ground black pepper to taste

4 ounces sliced prosciutto (about 16 slices)

16 fresh sage leaves

4 tablespoons olive oil

8 cloves Caramelized Garlic (page 8), pureed

1 lemon, sliced

¼ cup white wine

Preheat the grill.

Lay the veal slices out on a flat surface and sprinkle with pepper. Cover each with a slice of prosciutto and a sage leaf. Roll up each veal slice and secure with a toothpick or twine. Make a paste from 3 tablespoons of olive oil and the garlic. Brush the veal rolls with the garlic/oil paste and sear on a hot grill for 2 minutes on each side. At the same time, grill the lemon slices until lightly brown on each side.

Heat the wine in a sauté pan, add the veal rolls, cover, and simmer for 1 minute. Remove the toothpicks or twine and arrange the veal rolls on a serving dish. Drizzle with the remaining olive oil and serve with grilled lemon slices.

Chicken Cacciatore

Cacciatore comes from the Italian word *cacciore*, "to hunt." This recipe is made in the style of the hunter who would start the stew cooking, go out into the woods, and come back to find dinner ready and waiting.

GRILL TEMPERATURE
high, then medium

Makes
4 servings

One 3-pound chicken, cut into 10 pieces

2 tablespoons olive oil

1 onion, sliced, grilled (page 9), and chopped

10 plum tomatoes, grilled (page 9) and chopped

1/4 cup dry red wine

8 cloves Caramelized Garlic (page 8), pureed

4 fresh basil leaves, chopped

1 teaspoon dried oregano

2 bay leaves

Freshly ground black pepper to taste

Preheat the grill.

Brush the chicken parts with the olive oil. Sear on the grill for 4 to 5 minutes on each side and remove. Place the chicken in a large saucepan with the onion, tomato, wine, and garlic and bring to a boil. Add the basil, oregano, bay leaves, and pepper and stir well. Lower the temperature, cover, and cook until the chicken is tender, about 30 minutes. Discard the bay leaves before serving.

Italy

Chicken Piccata

GRILL
TEMPERATURE
**high, then
medium-high**

**Makes
4 servings**

*P*iccata is the classic Italian technique of sautéing thinly sliced floured meats, then dressing them with lemon juice and parsley. I grill the chicken first, then add artichoke hearts and olives.

Four 6-ounce chicken breasts

3 tablespoons olive oil

8 canned artichoke hearts

1/4 cup dry white wine

6 cloves Caramelized Garlic (page 8), pureed

Juice of 2 lemons

1/4 cup sliced green olives

1 tablespoon chopped fresh Italian parsley

Freshly ground black pepper to taste

Preheat the grill.

Brush the chicken breasts with the olive oil and sear on a hot grill for 3 to 4 minutes on each side.

Place the chicken, artichoke hearts, wine, garlic, lemon juice, and olives in a large skillet. Bring to a boil, lower the heat, and simmer for 4 to 5 minutes, stirring occasionally. Add the parsley and pepper and stir well.

Chicken Scarpariello

GRILL
TEMPERATURE
medium

**Makes
4 servings**

Many Italian dishes are named for the people who supposedly invented them: marinara sauce was cooked by sailors, carbonara sauce was prepared in the mines, puttanesca was a favorite of the ladies of the night, and scarpariello was made by the local shoemaker.

One 2¹⁄₂-pound chicken

3 tablespoons olive oil

Juice of 2 lemons

2 heads Caramelized Garlic (page 8), pureed

1 tablespoon dried rosemary, crushed

1 tablespoon chopped fresh parsley

Freshly ground black pepper to taste

¹⁄₂ cup dry white wine

1 bunch arugula, cleaned and trimmed

Preheat the grill.

Truss the chicken and rub with 1 tablespoon of olive oil. Cook the whole chicken on the grill over medium heat with the cover down, or on a rotisserie. Keep turning the chicken until it is brown on all sides, 20 to 25 minutes. Remove the chicken and cool for at least 1 hour. Cut the chicken into ten pieces. Place the chicken in a bowl with the lemon juice, 1 head pureed garlic, rosemary, parsley, and pepper, toss well, and marinate for 30 minutes in the refrigerator.

Heat the remaining olive oil in a large sauté pan over high heat and add the chicken. Cook the chicken, tossing constantly until the chicken crisps. Add the wine, remaining garlic, and arugula and continue cooking for 1 minute.

Italy

Chicken with Smoked Ham and Fontina

Although fontina cheese is made in the United States, Denmark, and Sweden, I like the sharper taste of the Italian variety. Fontina melts to a smooth, creamy consistency.

**Makes
4 servings**

Four 6-ounce chicken cutlets

2 tablespoons olive oil

1/2 teaspoon Tabasco

1/4 cup Chicken Stock (page 11)

1/4 cup dry white wine

One 12-ounce ham steak, grilled (page 10), boned, and cut into 4 very thin pieces

4 slices fontina cheese

4 fresh basil leaves

Freshly ground black pepper to taste

1 lemon, sliced thin and grilled

Preheat the Grill.

Brush the chicken cutlets with the olive oil and season with Tabasco. Sear the cutlets for 2 minutes over high heat; turn and cook 2 minutes longer over medium heat. Heat the stock and wine in a sauté pan. Top the cutlets with the grilled ham, fontina, and basil and place in the pan. Return the pan to the cooler edge of the grill and cook until the chicken is done, about 4 to 5 minutes longer. Sprinkle with pepper, and top each with a lemon slice.

Potatoes with Salt Cod

Salting cod is an age-old method of preserving this fish for use during the winter months. As long as the cod is soaked properly, the rest is easy.

GRILL
TEMPERATURE
high, then
medium

Makes
6 servings

½ pound salt cod

6 russet potatoes, sliced ½-inch thick and grilled (page 9)

2 long hot peppers, halved and seeded

¼ cup olive oil

Juice of 1 lemon

1 teaspoon dried thyme

1 teaspoon freshly ground black pepper

1 onion, sliced and grilled (page 9)

1 rib celery, finely chopped

Soak the salted cod in cold water for 24 hours, changing the water every 5 to 6 hours. Drain and set aside for 30 minutes.

Brush the potatoes and peppers with 2 tablespoons of olive oil and sear on both sides on a hot grill. Brush the cod with 1 tablespoon of olive oil and season on both sides with lemon juice, thyme, and black pepper. Grill the cod over medium heat for 3 minutes on one side; turn and grill for 4 minutes on the second side. Cut the pepper and potato into strips and serve with the cod and grilled onion slices; top with chopped celery and the remaining olive oil.

Italy

Scaloppine of Chicken Fontina

Don't use a meat mallet with teeth to pound the chicken breasts because there's a chance they could tear. Rather, use a flat meat mallet or chef's knife.

Makes
4 servings

Four 6-ounce boneless and skinless chicken breasts

4 tablespoons olive oil

1 teaspoon Tabasco

6 small, hard French rolls

1 head Caramelized Garlic (page 8), pureed

8 ounces prosciutto or smoked ham, sliced thin

8 ounces fontina or Swiss cheese, sliced thin

2 tablespoons coarsely chopped fresh basil leaves

1 recipe Scaloppine of Chicken Fontina Sauce (recipe follows)

Preheat the grill or side burner.

Cut each chicken breast into three pieces on an angle. Lightly pound the chicken with a flat meat mallet until 1/4 inch thick. Marinate the chicken in 2 tablespoons of olive oil and the Tabasco for 30 minutes in the refrigerator. Place the chicken on a very hot grill and sear for 2 minutes on each side.

Cut the French rolls in half, brush the cut sides with the remaining 2 tablespoons of olive oil, and rub them with the caramelized garlic. Lightly toast the rolls, cut sides down, on the grill.

Divide the prosciutto and cheese into twelve equal portions. Cover the grilled chicken pieces with the prosciutto and cheese. Place the chicken back on a medium grill until the cheese begins to melt. Serve the chicken, open-faced, on the toasted rolls. Serve the sauce on the side.

Scaloppine of Chicken Fontina Sauce

1 teaspoon olive oil

1 small onion, sliced, grilled (page 9), and chopped fine

1/2 cup plain yogurt

2 tablespoons Dijon mustard

1/2 teaspoon Tabasco

**Makes
1 cup**

Heat the olive oil in a small skillet and add the grilled onion. Cook over low heat until the onion caramelizes and is well browned. Place in a bowl with the yogurt, mustard, and Tabasco and mix well.

Italy

Bronzino

*B*ronzino is the Italian name for a sea bass that spends part of its life in freshwater. Roasting the fish in salt locks in all the moisture, resulting in a sweet taste and delicate texture.

1 tablespoon olive oil

One 3- to 3½-pound whole sea bass, with scales left on

1 teaspoon Tabasco

1 head Caramelized Garlic (page 8), pureed

4 cups coarse salt

1 recipe Bronzino Sauce (recipe follows)

Preheat the grill.

Grease a large ovenproof pan with the olive oil. Season the fish with the Tabasco and the garlic and place it in the pan. Cover the fish completely with the salt and set the pan over a medium fire for 45 to 60 minutes with the grill cover down. When done, the fish should flake easily when tested with a fork. Remove the fish and scrape away the salt. Peel off the skin with the scales and remove the fillet. Serve with Bronzino Sauce.

Bronzino Sauce

This sauce is both sweet and tart, piquant and unctuous all at the same time.

GRILL
TEMPERATURE
medium-high

Makes
1 cup

1 tablespoon olive oil

¼ onion, sliced, grilled (page 9), and chopped

½ cup dry white wine

1 tablespoon raisins

2 tablespoons butter, softened and cut into chunks

1 tablespoon coarsely chopped fresh parsley

Juice of ½ lemon

Preheat the grill or side burner.

Heat the olive oil in a sauté pan; add the onion and cook for 2 minutes. Add the wine and raisins and cook 2 minutes longer. Stirring continuously, quickly stir in the butter until it melts. Add the parsley and lemon juice and blend well.

Italy

Red Snapper, Calabrese Style

GRILL
TEMPERATURE
medium-high

**Makes
4 servings**

Calabria is the foot of the boot on the map of Italy. It is the region known for *fritto misto,* a mixed dish of fried fish and vegetables. This grilled version results in a crispy fish.

Two 1½-pound whole red snappers, gutted and scaled

1 tablespoon Tabasco

¼ cup olive oil

4 tablespoons (½ stick) butter

8 cloves Caramelized Garlic (page 8), pureed

¼ cup sliced black olives

Juice and zest of 1 lemon

1 tablespoon capers or chopped green olives

1 tablespoon chopped fresh parsley

Freshly ground black pepper to taste

Preheat the grill.

Brush the fish with the Tabasco and then with the olive oil. Grill the fish for 4 to 5 minutes, turn, and grill on the other side for 4 to 5 minutes. Remove the fish and keep it warm on a serving platter.

On the grill or side burner, heat the butter in a small saucepan. When the butter begins to brown, stir in the garlic, olives, lemon juice and zest, capers, parsley, and pepper. Heat the sauce through and pour over the fish.

Tuna and Tomatoes, Sardinian Style

Sardinia is an island off the coast of Italy where fishing is a way of life. When the tuna are running, most families have tuna for dinner many nights in a row. The tuna in this recipe is quickly seared for only a few minutes on each side, but you can cook it to your liking.

GRILL TEMPERATURE
high, then medium-high, then high

Makes 4 servings

Four 8-ounce tuna steaks

4 tablespoons olive oil

12 plum tomatoes, cut vertically through the stem ends

1 onion, sliced

¼ cup dry white wine

8 cloves Caramelized Garlic (page 8), pureed

4 tablespoons chopped green olives

2 tablespoons chopped fresh basil

Freshly ground black pepper to taste

Preheat the grill.

Brush the tuna with 2 tablespoons of olive oil, place it on a hot grill, and sear for 2 minutes on each side. Remove the tuna, set it aside, and keep it warm.

Brush the tomatoes and onion with the remaining 2 tablespoons of olive oil. Grill the vegetables for 2 minutes; turn and grill 2 minutes longer. Remove and coarsely chop the vegetables. Combine them with the wine, garlic, olives, and basil and toss on high heat for 1 minute in a sauté pan. Season with pepper and pile on top of the tuna steaks.

Clam Pie

This is a spinoff of quiche. If you want to make a lower-fat version, substitute 2 eggs and 4 egg whites for the 4 eggs. Although this pie tastes best when made with fresh clams, canned clams can be used in a pinch.

1 cup clams, drained (if canned) and chopped

1 cup finely chopped cooked potato

1 green bell pepper, grilled (page 8) and chopped

½ onion, grilled (page 9) and chopped

4 ounces ham, grilled (page 10) and chopped

4 cloves Caramelized Garlic (page 8), pureed

4 eggs, lightly beaten

1 cup half-and-half

1 teaspoon Tabasco

1 teaspoon dried thyme

Freshly ground black pepper to taste

2 tablespoons melted butter

1 cup finely crushed soda crackers

Preheat the grill.

In a medium bowl, combine the clams, potato, green pepper, onion, ham, and garlic.

In a separate bowl, mix the eggs with the half-and-half, Tabasco, thyme, and black pepper.

Spread the melted butter evenly in the bottom of a 9-inch pie plate and top with the cracker crumbs. Spread the clam mixture evenly over the cracker crumbs and pour in the egg mixture. Place the pan over a medium fire for 5 minutes, then reduce the temperature to low and bake for 20 to 25 minutes longer with the grill cover down. If the bottom of the pie begins to darken before the pie is cooked, move the pie to the top shelf of the grill or place a few bricks on the grill and put the pie on top of them.

Grilled Lobster Spedini

If your idea of a grilled cheese sandwich is a slice of cheese between two slices of bread, this recipe will change your mind forever. Substitute shrimp, grilled ham, or even grilled vegetables for the lobster if you like.

One 1- to 1¼-pound lobster, split and cleaned
12 slices day-old white bread
8 thin slices mozzarella cheese
4 fresh basil leaves, chopped
2 tablespoons olive oil
2 tablespoons butter

Batter

3 eggs, well beaten
2 tablespoons milk
2 tablespoons grated Parmesan cheese
1 teaspoon chopped fresh Italian parsley
½ teaspoon Tabasco
Freshly ground black pepper to taste

Preheat the grill.

Grill the lobster for 6 to 7 minutes, turning once. Remove and cool. Remove the meat from the tail and claw and divide it into four portions.

Place a slice of cheese and a portion of the lobster meat on each of four slices of bread. Top each with a second slice of bread, a slice of cheese, some basil, and a third slice of bread. Flatten the sandwiches by pressing them down with the bottom of a skillet.

Heat the olive oil and butter in a sauté pan.

Combine the batter ingredients in a medium bowl and mix well.

Dip the sandwiches, one at a time, into the batter and quickly brown them on both sides in the pan. Remove from the pan and place on the grill until the cheese melts, about 1 minute.

Garlic-Lemon Oil

2 tablespoons olive oil

Juice of 1 lemon

3 cloves Caramelized Garlic (page 8), pureed

1 teaspoon chopped fresh Italian parsley

To make the sauce, heat the olive oil in a small sauté pan. Add the lemon, garlic, and parsley and stir until the mixture is smooth. Drizzle the sauce over the sandwiches.

FRANCE

If the difficult techniques so often associated with French cooking have turned you away from preparing French food, consider the no-fuss dishes in this chapter. From Seared Breast of Duck with Greens and Grilled Fruit and Potatoes au Gratin to Provençal Sauce and Oyster Stew, you'll see that it isn't necessary to be a professional chef to come up with professional-tasting, French-inspired dishes made right on the grill.

In the words of brilliant culinary authority Auguste Escoffier, who grew up in the land of *feu de bois,* where the best food is prepared over charcoal and vine-cutting fires perfumed with a handful of fresh herbs: *"Faites simple"*—make it simple.

Hot Smoked-Shrimp Bisque

Whether you add the heavy cream because it tastes so good or the instant mashed potato flakes to cut down on calories, the final version will be thick and creamy.

2 pounds medium shrimp

8 cups Fish Stock (page 12)

4 tablespoons olive oil

1 onion, sliced, grilled (page 9), and finely chopped

1 rib celery, chopped fine

3 cloves Caramelized Garlic (page 8), pureed

1 teaspoon sweet paprika

1 teaspoon ground thyme

1 teaspoon Tabasco

2 tablespoons all-purpose flour

8 plum tomatoes, grilled (page 9) and chopped

Pinch ground nutmeg

Freshly ground black pepper to taste

**1 cup heavy cream, or (for a lower-fat version) ¹/₂ cup instant
   mashed potato flakes**

Peel and devein the shrimp; reserve the shells.

Preheat the grill.

Place the shrimp shells on the grill and cook them until they become crisp and red. Heat the fish stock, add the grilled shells, and simmer for 10 minutes. Strain the stock and discard the shells.

Meanwhile, place an iron smoker box filled with fruitwood or hickory in the corner of the hot grill and wait until the wood begins to smolder. Brush the shrimp with 2 tablespoons of olive oil, place on the grill, lower the grill hood, and smoke for 4 minutes. Do not overcook the shrimp. Remove the shrimp and chop half of them into small pieces.

Heat the remaining 2 tablespoons of olive oil in a stockpot or soup kettle. Add the onion, celery, garlic, paprika, thyme, and Tabasco and sauté for 2 to 3 minutes. Stir in the flour and cook 1 minute. Add the tomatoes and cook for 5 minutes. Add the hot stock, shrimp, nutmeg, and pepper. Heat the soup through and stir in the cream or the mashed potato flakes. Simmer for 2 minutes and serve.

Seared Breast of Duck with Greens and Grilled Fruit

GRILL
TEMPERATURE
medium-high

**Makes
4 servings**

The French have been known to work miracles with duck, thanks to the superior quality of the birds from the Rouen region. In the United States, the best ducks are the white Pekin from Long Island. It is extremely important to boil the marinade before brushing it on the duck breasts.

1/2 **cup orange juice**

1 tablespoon chopped fresh mint

1 tablespoon balsamic vinegar

1 tablespoon honey

1 teaspoon Tabasco

2 duck breasts, with skin attached

Cooked greens such as spinach, chard, or kale, about 2 cups

Grilled fruit such as peaches, oranges, apples, or pears (page 10), about 2 cups

1/2 **cup Vinaigrette for Duck (recipe follows)**

Mix the orange juice, mint, vinegar, honey, and Tabasco in a resealable plastic bag. Add the duck breasts and marinate for 24 hours in the refrigerator. Remove the duck breasts from the marinade and pat them dry with paper towels.

Preheat the grill.

Place the duck breasts, skin sides down, on a hot grill and cook for 2 to 3 minutes. Turn and cook 3 to 4 minutes longer.

Boil the marinade for 2 minutes and brush the ducks several times with the mixture while they're cooking.

Allow the meat to rest for 5 minutes, then slice it thin on an angle. Place the cooked greens on four dishes and top evenly with the sliced duck. Garnish with grilled fruit and sprinkle 2 tablespoons of Vinaigrette for Duck on each serving.

Vinaigrette for Duck

**Makes
1 cup**

⅔ cup orange juice

⅓ cup olive oil

3 cloves Caramelized Garlic (page 8), pureed

1 tablespoon Dijon mustard

1 teaspoon chopped fresh mint

Freshly ground black pepper to taste

Combine all of the ingredients in a medium bowl and mix well. Set aside for 1 hour before using.

France

Veal American

A veal medallion is small, coin-shaped, and very tender.

1½ pounds veal from the leg, sliced very thin

3 tablespoons olive oil

2 shallots, chopped

1 cup Chicken Stock (page 11)

½ cup tomato sauce

¼ cup white wine

1 tablespoon chopped fresh basil

½ pound large shrimp

½ cup heavy cream

Freshly ground black pepper to taste

Preheat the grill.

Brush the veal with 1 tablespoon of the olive oil. Grill for 2 minutes, turn, and grill for 1 minute longer. Remove and set aside. Add 1 tablespoon of the olive oil in a sauté pan and sauté the shallots 1 minute. Add the chicken stock, tomato sauce, white wine, and basil to the pan and cook until reduced by one half.

Brush the shrimp with the remaining tablespoon of olive oil, sear on the grill for 4 to 5 minutes, and add to the tomato sauce mixture. Simmer for 2 minutes and add the cream. Heat through, sprinkle with pepper, and serve at once.

Tuna Steaks with Honey-Mustard Marinade

Tuna's full flavor is sturdy enough to balance the sweetness of this honey-mustard marinade. This tastes best served cold or at room temperature.

GRILL TEMPERATURE
medium-high

**Makes
4 servings**

¼ **cup vegetable oil**

Juice of 1 lemon

2 **tablespoons cider vinegar**

2 **tablespoons honey**

2 **tablespoons water**

½ **teaspoon dry mustard**

¼ **teaspoon Tabasco**

¼ **teaspoon dried oregano**

¼ **teaspoon dried basil**

¼ **teaspoon dried parsley**

¼ **teaspoon sweet paprika**

¼ **teaspoon freshly ground black pepper**

Four 8-ounce tuna steaks

Combine all of the ingredients except the tuna in a large shallow bowl and mix well. Add the tuna and refrigerate for 2 hours.

Preheat the grill.

Grill the tuna for 3 to 4 minutes, turn, and grill 4 to 5 minutes longer. Be careful not to overcook the tuna; it can be slightly pink in the center.

France

Provençal Sauce for Fish

This sauce will go well with swordfish, salmon, tuna, or halibut steak. Reserve any accumulated juices when cooking the fish and add them to the sauce. This makes enough for four 8-ounce pieces of fish.

½ cup bread crumbs

1 red bell pepper, charred on the outside (page 8), peeled, and chopped

1 head Caramelized Garlic (page 8), pureed

4 tablespoons olive oil

Juices from grilled fish

Soak the bread crumbs in 1 cup tepid water until they become moist and squeeze out as much liquid as possible. Combine the bread crumbs with the pepper, garlic, olive oil, and fish juices and mix well.

Oyster Stew

The town of Oyster Bay on Long Island celebrates the oyster harvest with an annual oyster festival. You can celebrate in your own way with a quiet dinner for two featuring oysters and champagne.

GRILL
TEMPERATURE
medium-high

**Makes
4 servings**

2 slices bacon, chopped finely

8 small new potatoes, cut in half and boiled for 10 minutes

1 onion, sliced, grilled (page 9), and chopped

1 green bell pepper, grilled (page 8) and chopped

6 cloves Caramelized Garlic (page 8), pureed

One 12-ounce can ale

Oyster liquor from shucked oysters

2 scallions, chopped

1 tablespoon chopped fresh parsley

1 teaspoon dry mustard

1/2 teaspoon Tabasco

2 cups shucked oysters

2 tablespoons butter, cut into small pieces

Oyster crackers

Preheat the grill or side burner.

Cook the bacon in a large saucepan until it gives up its fat. Add the potato, onion, green pepper, and garlic and cook for 1 minute. Add the ale, oyster liquor, scallion, parsley, and mustard and simmer for 5 minutes. Add the oysters; in about 2 minutes, they will plump and the edges will begin to curl. Add the butter and quickly stir until it melts. Serve immediately with the oyster crackers.

France

Grilled Oysters in Tomato-Mussel Broth

GRILL
TEMPERATURE

**medium-high,
then low, then
medium-high**

Makes
4 servings

It is said that the best oysters come from the Baltic or Dutch coastline. Whether or not this is true is up for debate. I've cooked some pretty good oysters from the Atlantic-Gulf coast, as well as Olympia oysters from Washington's Puget Sound.

1 cup white wine

1 onion, sliced and grilled (page 9)

1 head Caramelized Garlic (page 8), pureed

1 tablespoon chopped fresh thyme

2 pounds mussels, scrubbed and debearded

4 plum tomatoes, grilled (page 9) and chopped

3 tablespoons butter, cut into small pieces

1 teaspoon Tabasco

2 dozen oysters, scrubbed, on the half shell

One 10-ounce bag of spinach, chopped

Preheat the grill or side burner.

Place the white wine, onion, garlic, and thyme in a large saucepan. Add the mussels, cover, and bring to a boil, shaking the pan occasionally. Remove the cover after 5 minutes and discard any mussels that have not opened. Remove the mussels and strain the liquid into a small saucepan Add the mussels and tomatoes to the liquid, bring to a boil, and cook until the liquid is reduced by half. Lower the heat and add the butter a piece at a time, stirring constantly, until it melts. Stir in the Tabasco.

Place the oysters on the grill, lower the lid, and cook for 2 to 3 minutes on medium-high. Remove the oysters from their shells and serve with the tomato-mussel broth on a bed of chopped spinach.

Lyonnaise Potatoes

Some consider Lyons the gastronomic capital of France. Whether or not you agree, this classic potato-and-onion dish is easily one of Lyons's best.

> **3 russet potatoes, grilled (page 9) or boiled**
>
> **2 tablespoons butter**
>
> **6 cloves Caramelized Garlic (page 8), pureed**
>
> **2 onions, thinly sliced and grilled (page 9)**
>
> **1 teaspoon dried thyme**
>
> **1 teaspoon dried sage**
>
> **¹/₂ teaspoon Tabasco**
>
> **Pinch ground nutmeg**
>
> **Freshly ground black pepper to taste**
>
> **1 cup hot Chicken Stock (page 11) or vegetable stock**
>
> **2 tablespoons grated Parmesan cheese**

Preheat the grill.

Peel and slice the cooked potatoes ¹/₄ inch thick. Melt the butter in a heatproof casserole and add the garlic. Alternate layers of the potato and onion slices in the casserole dish, seasoning each layer with thyme, sage, Tabasco, nutmeg, and pepper. Pour in the hot stock and sprinkle evenly with the grated cheese. Cover the dish with a tight-fitting lid or aluminum foil and grill for 10 minutes with the lid down. Uncover the casserole, close the grill lid, and cook for 5 minutes.

Potatoes au Gratin

When a dish is called *au gratin*, it usually means that it's topped with either bread crumbs or cheese (this one has both) and cooked until the top becomes brown and crispy.

GRILL TEMPERATURE
medium

Makes 6 servings

4 russet potatoes, grilled (page 9) or boiled

1 onion, sliced, grilled (page 9), and chopped

4 cloves garlic, sliced thin

¹⁄₂ cup shredded sharp Cheddar cheese

¹⁄₂ cup shredded Swiss cheese

¹⁄₄ cup grated Parmesan cheese

3 tablespoons butter, melted

2 tablespoons all-purpose flour

2 cups hot milk, half-and-half, or cream

3 tablespoons bread crumbs

1 teaspoon Tabasco

¹⁄₂ teaspoon sweet paprika

Pinch ground nutmeg

Freshly ground black pepper to taste

Preheat the grill.

Peel the potatoes and slice them thin. In a heatproof 2-quart casserole, layer half of the potato, onion, garlic, Cheddar, Swiss, and Parmesan cheeses, butter, and flour. Repeat the layer. Pour the hot milk over the potato mixture. Combine the bread crumbs, Tabasco, paprika, nutmeg, and pepper and sprinkle over the potato mixture. Cover the dish with a tight-fitting lid or aluminum foil and grill for 18 to 20 minutes with the lid down. Uncover the dish and cook for 5 minutes with the grill lid down.

France

Swiss Chard with Honey

A member of the beet family, this green tastes more like spinach. Red Swiss chard has a stronger flavor than the lighter variety, and either works well here.

1 bunch Swiss chard, washed, dried, and stemmed

2 tablespoons butter, melted, or olive oil

1 onion, sliced, grilled (page 9), and chopped

Juice of 1 lemon

2 tablespoons honey

2 tablespoons raisins

Freshly ground black pepper to taste

Pinch ground nutmeg

Preheat the grill or side burner.

Blanch the Swiss chard stems in boiling water until slightly tender, about 4 minutes. Add the leaves and cook for 30 seconds. Drain the chard well and toss with the butter or oil. Place the chard on the grill and cook for 1 minute, tossing constantly. Remove the chard and place it in a saucepan on the grill or side burner. Add the onion, lemon juice, honey, raisins, pepper, and nutmeg, and mix well. Heat through and serve.

SPAIN

With their extended shoreline and rugged, mountainous interior, Spaniards enjoy a cornucopia of seafood and meat. Paella, probably Spain's most famous dish, is always different, depending on where you're eating it. It can be made with seafood and chicken, seafood and pork, pork and chicken, or even vegetarian ingredients. The only common denominator is the rice grown on Spain's eastern coast. The distinctive rustic flavors found in the cuisine of Spain adapt themselves very readily to the grill, especially Charred Cod with Aïoli and Chicken in Garlic Sauce. And, while it's distinctly different from Mexican cuisine, this gustatory adventure uses the same name: fiesta!

Grilled Pork Threads

GRILL
TEMPERATURE
high

**Makes
4 servings**

The running of the bulls in Pamplona may be the best-known Spanish festival, but to me, the Day of the Dead, or All Souls' Day, celebrated in early November, marks an occasion any grillmeister would appreciate—the beginning of the hog butchering season. Here is a delicious way to prepare the most tender cut of all.

1 pound pork tenderloin, sliced ¼ inch thick and pounded thin

¼ cup Pork Spice Rub (recipe follows)

2 tablespoons olive oil

Juice of 1 lemon

4 flour tortillas

1 avocado, peeled and sliced

Slice the cutlets into 1-inch-wide strips. Sprinkle the Pork Spice Rub over the strips, mix well, and refrigerate for at least 2 hours. Shake off any excess spice mixture and thread the meat onto skewers. Brush with a mixture of the olive oil and lemon juice.

Preheat the grill.

Cook the meat for 2 minutes on each side. Grill the tortillas for 30 seconds on each side. Remove the meat from the skewers and place on the tortillas with a few slices of avocado. Roll up the tortillas and serve.

Pork Spice Rub

2 dried chilies, chopped

1 teaspoon sweet paprika

1 teaspoon ground cumin

1 teaspoon ground coriander

1 teaspoon black pepper

1 teaspoon garlic powder

1 teaspoon dried parsley

1 teaspoon dried oregano

1 teaspoon dried thyme

Makes almost ¼ cup

Combine all of the ingredients in a small bowl and mix well. Store in a tightly covered container.

Spain

Paella

GRILL
TEMPERATURE
**high, then
medium**

**Makes
4 servings**

Paella is to the Spaniards what jambalaya is to the Cajuns—soul food. There are as many recipes for paella as there are for pasta. This one is in the style of Valencia, an area of Spain rich in seafood.

One 2½-pound chicken, cut into 8 pieces

4 tablespoons olive oil

2 cups long-grain or arborio rice

1 red bell pepper, grilled (page 8) and chopped

1 green bell pepper, grilled (page 8) and chopped

4 plum tomatoes, grilled (page 9) and coarsely chopped

1 head Caramelized Garlic (page 8), pureed

1 teaspoon sweet paprika

3 bay leaves

4 cups hot Chicken Stock (page 11)

1 teaspoon Tabasco

½ teaspoon saffron threads, or 1 teaspoon turmeric

½ pound chorizo sausage, grilled for 5 minutes (page 10), cooled, and sliced

½ pound ¼-inch-thick ham or ham steak, grilled for 2 minutes (page 10) and diced

12 mussels, scrubbed and debearded

8 littleneck clams

½ pound large shrimp, peeled, deveined, and grilled for 2 minutes

One 1½-pound lobster, split, cleaned, and grilled for 3 to 4 minutes

1 cup cooked chick-peas

½ cup green peas, fresh or frozen

¼ cup each sliced green and black olives

2 scallions with their tops, chopped

Preheat the grill.

Brush the chicken with 2 tablespoons of olive oil and grill for 8 to 10 minutes over high heat. Set aside.

In a paella pan or a large sauté pan with a tight-fitting cover, heat the remaining 2 tablespoons of olive oil. Add the rice, green and red peppers, tomato, garlic, paprika, and bay leaves and, stirring constantly, cook for 2 minutes, or until the rice is lightly toasted. Add the stock, Tabasco, and saffron, bring to a boil, and lower heat to a simmer.

Add the chicken pieces, sausage, ham, mussels, and clams. Cover the pan tightly and cook for 5 minutes. Add the shrimp, lobster, chick-peas, green peas, olives, and scallion and cook until the rice is tender, about 5 minutes. Remove from the heat and set aside for 5 minutes. Discard the bay leaves and serve.

Chicken in Garlic Sauce

GRILL
TEMPERATURE
**medium, then
high**

**Makes
4 servings**

Cook the chicken slowly to caramelize the outside. Two heads of garlic may seem like a lot, but as the garlic cooks, it mellows in flavor.

One 2½-pound chicken, cut into 8 pieces

2 heads Caramelized Garlic (page 8), pureed

Freshly ground black pepper to taste

2 tablespoons olive oil

¼ cup dry white wine

2 tablespoons coarsely chopped fresh oregano, parsley, or thyme

Rub the chicken with the garlic puree, sprinkle with pepper, and refrigerate for 1 hour.

Preheat the grill.

Brush the chicken with olive oil and grill on medium heat, turning several times, until the skin browns, 20 to 25 minutes. Move the chicken to a hotter part of the grill to crisp the skin. The total cooking time should be approximately 30 to 35 minutes. Place the cooked chicken in a hot sauté pan, pour the wine over the chicken, and sprinkle with the fresh herbs.

Charred Cod with Aïoli

This Basque dish features the garlicky mayonnaise traditionally served with fish and meat dishes. If cod is unavailable, use halibut or any other firm white fish. Leaving the skin on the fish helps keep it from falling apart on the grill.

GRILL
TEMPERATURE
high, then
medium-high

Makes
4 servings

> 1½ pounds cod fillet, with skin attached, scales removed
>
> 4 tablespoons olive oil
>
> ½ teaspoon freshly ground black pepper

Aïoli

> 1 red bell pepper, grilled (page 8) and seeded
>
> 1 head Caramelized Garlic (page 8), pureed
>
> Juice of 1 lemon
>
> ½ teaspoon Tabasco
>
> 1 cup mayonnaise

Preheat the grill.

Brush one side of the cod with half the olive oil and sprinkle with half the pepper. Place the fish, oil side down, on the grill over high heat for 3 minutes. Brush the other side of the fish with the remaining oil, sprinkle with the remaining pepper, turn, and cook 4 minutes longer. Serve with aïoli.

To make the aïoli, place the roasted pepper, garlic puree, lemon juice, and Tabasco in a blender or food processor and process for 1 minute. Stir in the mayonnaise. Refrigerate until ready to serve.

Spain

GERMANY

German food is hefty and hearty, lots of full-bodied flavors that stick to the ribs like one-dish soups, goulash, and rouladens. Dishes that traditionally take hours to marinate have been adapted to the grill and take only a fraction of the time. Try your hand at smoking a duck with a tasty apple stuffing. Rather than marinate a sauerbraten 3 or 4 days, try our version of Sauerbraten Steak marinated for only a day. Sauerkraut Pie is one way of giving this humble vegetable star billing. And you'll become a champion Spätzle-maker in no time following our directions. And, as a fitting finale, treat yourself to Apple Strudel full of plump apple slices flavored with brandy, cinnamon, and nutmeg.

Lentil Soup

Popular in Europe and a staple throughout the Middle East, lentils make a hearty one-dish meal in just under an hour.

½ pound lentils
4 tablespoons olive oil
2 slices bacon, chopped
1 onion, sliced, grilled (page 9), and chopped
1 head Caramelized Garlic (page 8), pureed
½ cup chopped celery
½ cup chopped carrot
1 slice ham steak, grilled (page 10) and diced
6 cups chicken or vegetable stock
2 tablespoons cider vinegar
1 teaspoon Tabasco
½ teaspoon dried thyme
¼ teaspoon freshly ground black pepper
Pinch ground nutmeg
1 large potato, peeled and diced
1 recipe Grilled Rye Croutons (recipe follows)

Rinse the lentils in cool water and remove any small stones or twigs.

Heat a large stockpot on the grill or side burner. Add 2 tablespoons of the olive oil and the bacon and cook until the bacon is light brown. Add the onion, garlic, celery, carrot, and ham steak and cook for 2 to 3 minutes, stirring once or twice. Add the stock, vinegar, Tabasco, thyme, black pepper, and nutmeg and bring to a boil. Lower the heat and simmer for 45 minutes, or until the lentils are tender.

Meanwhile, brush the potato with the remaining 2 tablespoons of olive oil and place it on a hot grill for 3 to 4 minutes on each side, or until tender. Stir the potato into the soup and serve with the croutons.

Grilled Rye Croutons

4 slices day-old rye bread

2 tablespoons melted butter

1 tablespoon grated Parmesan cheese

1 teaspoon freshly ground black pepper

$\frac{1}{2}$ teaspoon sweet paprika

$\frac{1}{4}$ teaspoon dry mustard

GRILL
TEMPERATURE
medium

Makes
1 cup

Preheat the grill.

Brush the rye bread slices with the melted butter on both sides, place on the grill, and lightly toast on both sides. Remove the bread and cut it into $\frac{1}{2}$-inch pieces. Combine the Parmesan cheese, pepper, paprika, and mustard in a small bowl and, while the bread is still hot, add it to the bowl and toss until well coated.

Germany

Potato-Cabbage Soup

Bavarians have a close emotional relationship with cabbage, whether it's braised, fried, steamed, boiled, cooked in soups, or shredded in salads. This hearty, rustic cabbage soup is great for warming chilled bones.

4 slices bacon, chopped

2 cups shredded cabbage

1 onion, sliced, grilled (page 9), and chopped

6 cloves Caramelized Garlic (page 8), pureed

2 tablespoons all-purpose flour

6 cups hot Chicken Stock (page 11)

2 cups peeled and diced potato

1 smoked ham hock

2 bay leaves

1 teaspoon dried thyme

Pinch ground nutmeg

Freshly ground black pepper to taste

1 cup heavy cream or half-and-half (optional)

Preheat the grill or side burner.

Cook the bacon in a soup kettle or Dutch oven over low heat for 2 to 3 minutes. Add the cabbage, onion, and garlic, and cook until the cabbage wilts, 2 to 3 minutes. Add the flour and cook 1 minute. Add the hot stock, potato, ham hock, bay leaves, thyme, and nutmeg. Bring the soup to a boil, lower the heat, and simmer for 1 hour. Remove the ham hock, pick the meat off the bone, chop it, and return it to the pot. Season the soup with black pepper.

If desired, puree one third of the soup, return to the pot, and stir in the cream.

Spätzle

The Italians eat pasta, the Chinese eat rice, and the Germans eat spätzle. These tiny noodles literally translated as "little sparrow," are traditionally served as a side dish with sauce or gravy.

GRILL TEMPERATURE
medium-high

Makes
4 servings

3 cups all-purpose flour

4 eggs, lightly beaten

1 teaspoon finely chopped fresh parsley

1 teaspoon salt

1/2 teaspoon Tabasco

Pinch ground nutmeg

Freshly ground black pepper to taste

Combine the flour, eggs, parsley, salt, Tabasco, nutmeg, and pepper in a large bowl. Add approximately 2 cups of water, a little at a time, and mix until the dough begins to bubble and does not adhere to the spoon. Set the dough aside to rest for 10 minutes.

Bring a large pot of water to a boil on a grill or side burner. Force the dough through a spätzle strainer or colander with large holes, allowing the pieces to fall directly into the water. Remove the spätzle as soon as they rise to the surface, and drop them into a bowl of cold water. After a few minutes, drain them and place them in warm water until ready to serve.

The dough can also be rolled out on a flat wet surface, cut into strips, and cooked as above.

continued

Variations:

- Combine the spätzle with 1 pound grilled and chopped ham steak.
- Add 2 cups grilled and chopped mushrooms with the spätzle.
- Serve the spätzle with 1 pound grilled bratwurst.
- Add the spätzle to soups, stews, and casseroles.

Grilled Hungarian Goulash

GRILL TEMPERATURE
high, then low

**Makes
6 servings**

A goulash, or *gulyás*, as it is known in its native Hungary, is a one-pot dish made with beef and flavored with paprika. Serve it over buttered noodles or boiled potatoes.

2 pounds bottom round or chuck stew, cut into 1-inch pieces

2 tablespoons sweet paprika

1 teaspoon dried thyme

1 teaspoon freshly ground black pepper

1 teaspoon Tabasco

1 tablespoon olive oil

1 onion, sliced, grilled (page 9), and chopped

1 head Caramelized Garlic (page 8), pureed

4 plum tomatoes, grilled (page 9) and chopped

1 cup tomato puree

1½ cups beef stock or Chicken Stock (page 11)

1 tablespoon red wine vinegar

2 bay leaves

1 cup crumbs from seeded rye bread

Preheat the grill.

Season the beef with the paprika, thyme, black pepper, and Tabasco. Brush the meat with the olive oil, place it on a very hot grill, and sear it on all sides for 5 to 6 minutes.

Remove the meat and place it in a 4- to 6-quart stockpot. Add the onion and garlic and heat for 2 minutes, stirring constantly. Add the tomato and tomato puree and cook for 5 minutes, stirring occasionally. Add the stock, vinegar, and bay leaves and simmer until the meat is tender, 1 to 1½ hours. Add the bread crumbs and stir well. Discard the bay leaves before serving.

Beef Rouladen

GRILL
TEMPERATURE
high, then low

**Makes
6 servings**

*R*ouladen are thin slices of meat wrapped around a filling of vegetables, cheese, or meat. When you cut the vegetables, make sure they are the same width as the meat.

2 pounds beef round

$^1/_2$ onion, sliced, grilled (page 9), and chopped

4 cloves Caramelized Garlic (page 8), pureed

$^1/_4$ cup bread crumbs

1 teaspoon dried thyme

1 teaspoon chopped fresh parsley

$^1/_2$ teaspoon Tabasco

Pinch ground nutmeg

6 thin carrot sticks, parboiled

6 thin pickle wedges

6 thin celery sticks

Freshly ground black pepper to taste

2 tablespoons olive oil

1 cup dry red wine

1 cup tomato sauce

1 cup beef stock

2 bay leaves

Preheat the grill.

Cut the beef round into six thin slices and pound them thin between sheets of wax paper with a meat pounder or the bottom of a heavy skillet. In a medium bowl, combine the onion, garlic, bread crumbs, thyme, parsley, Tabasco, and nutmeg.

Place the beef slices on a flat surface and spread the bread-crumb mixture evenly on the meat. Place a carrot stick, pickle wedge, and celery stick on the bottom edge of each meat slice and roll them up, securing them with tooth-picks or butcher twine. Season the outsides with black pepper.

Brush the *rouladen* with olive oil, place on a hot grill, and brown on all sides, 3 to 4 minutes. Combine the red wine, tomato sauce, beef stock, and bay leaves in a wide skillet and mix well. Place the *rouladen* in the sauce and simmer over low heat until tender, about 45 minutes. Remove the toothpicks and bay leaves before serving.

Sauerbraten Steak

GRILL
TEMPERATURE
high, then
low, then high

Makes
6 servings

Germans traditionally marinate sauerbraten for days and then cook it for hours. This version is made with round steaks and marinated for only one day. If you have a good sharp knife, you can cut the steaks from a bottom round roast yourself. Otherwise, ask your butcher to prepare them for you.

Six 10-ounce bottom round steaks

1 medium onion, sliced and grilled (page 9)

1 cup cider vinegar

$\frac{1}{2}$ cup sugar

$\frac{1}{2}$ cup red wine

$\frac{1}{2}$ cup sliced carrots

$\frac{1}{2}$ cup diced celery

5 cloves Caramelized Garlic (page 8), pureed

1 tablespoon prepared mustard

3 bay leaves

1 teaspoon whole black peppercorns

1 teaspoon dried thyme

2 tablespoons olive oil

1 cup beef stock

$\frac{1}{3}$ cup crushed gingersnaps

Preheat the grill.

Place the steaks on a very hot grill for 1 minute on each side, or until they're nicely browned. Remove from the grill and cool to room temperature. Combine the onion, vinegar, sugar, wine, carrot, celery, garlic, mustard, bay leaves, peppercorns, and thyme in a shallow nonreactive bowl and mix well. Add the cooled steaks and marinate for 24 hours in the refrigerator, turning several times.

Preheat the grill about 2 hours before serving.

Remove the meat from the marinade and pat dry. Heat the olive oil in a large skillet or Dutch oven on the grill or side burner. Add the steaks and heat them on both sides. Strain the marinade, add to the skillet with the stock, and simmer until the beef is fork-tender, about 1½ hours. Remove the steaks to a serving dish and keep warm. Add the gingersnaps to the sauce, raise the heat, and stir until they dissolve. Pour the sauce over the steaks.

Grilled Chicken Smothered with Mushrooms

Chanterelles are extremely popular in Germany. I like to make this dish with them but have found that they are not always available. Shiitakes work just as well. Once considered exotic, they are now available in most grocery stores nationwide. Originally from Japan and Korea, the meaty Shiitakes, or Chinese black mushrooms, are cultivated in the United States and available around the world.

2 pounds chicken cutlets, pounded ¹/₄ inch thick and cut in half

1 cup shiitake mushrooms, sliced

4 tablespoons olive oil

¹/₂ onion, sliced, grilled (page 9), and chopped

¹/₂ cup Chicken Stock (page 11)

¹/₄ cup half-and-half

1 teaspoon dried thyme

1 teaspoon dried parsley

1 teaspoon prepared mustard

Pinch ground nutmeg

Freshly ground black pepper to taste

Preheat the grill.

Brush the chicken and mushrooms with the olive oil and sear for 2 to 3 minutes on each side.

Combine the chicken, mushrooms, onion, stock, half-and-half, thyme, parsley, mustard, and nutmeg in a skillet and simmer for 2 minutes. Sprinkle with pepper and serve.

Pork Cutlets with Lemon Glaze

I like to serve this dish with an assortment of grilled fruit, including pears, peaches, and plums.

GRILL
TEMPERATURE
high

Makes
4 servings

1¹/₂ pounds pork loin cutlets, trimmed

Juice of 2 lemons

2 tablespoons olive oil

2 tablespoons honey

¹/₂ teaspoon dried rosemary

Freshly ground black pepper to taste

Place the cutlets between two sheets of wax paper and pound thin with a meat pounder or the bottom of a heavy skillet.

Combine the lemon juice, olive oil, honey, rosemary, and pepper in a small shallow bowl and mix well. Add the pork cutlets and refrigerate for 1 hour, turning the meat occasionally.

Preheat the grill.

Remove the meat from the marinade and grill for 2 to 3 minutes on each side, basting occasionally with the remaining marinade.

Germany

103

Smoked Duck with Apple Stuffing

PREPARE A SMOKER FOR
6 HOURS (CONSULT
MANUFACTURER'S
INSTRUCTIONS)

Makes
8 servings

When preparing the duck, remove the excess fat and save it to use in the stuffing or for frying potatoes. Serve with a spicy mustard or grilled fruits, such as peaches, plums, and cherries.

> **One 4- to 5-pound duck, washed and trussed**
> **¼ cup Poultry Rub (page 140)**
> **2 quarts hot apple cider**
> **2 cups vegetable peelings (onions, celery, carrots, garlic, parsnips, etc.)**
> **1 recipe Apple Stuffing (recipe follows)**

Rub the surface of the duck with the Poultry Rub. Cover lightly with plastic wrap and refrigerate for 24 hours.

Prepare the water smoker with the cider and vegetable peelings.

Keep the temperature at approximately 210°F. You'll need to add additional charcoal during the 6 hours of smoking. To do this, start a separate container of charcoal, allowing 30 minutes for it to become gray embers. Open the smoker door and add the charcoal.

Soak some wood chips for 30 minutes. After cooking the duck for 2½ hours, add the chips to the smoker. Use hickory or, for a milder flavor, fruitwood, such as apple or cherry, or vine clippings.

The duck is cooked when the temperature, taken with an instant-read thermometer, is 160°F. Remove the duck from the smoker and let it rest for 30 minutes before carving. Serve with Apple Stuffing.

Apple Stuffing

Although this stuffing is meant to go with the stuffed duck, it would be just as good with turkey. Smoking the apples first gives this stuffing a whole new dimension.

GRILL
TEMPERATURE
medium

**Makes
8 servings**

¼ cup margarine

3 Granny Smith apples, sliced, grilled (page 10), and diced

1 medium onion, sliced, grilled (page 9), and chopped

¼ cup diced celery

4 to 5 cloves Caramelized Garlic (page 8), pureed

4 cups cubed day-old rye bread

2 cups hot Chicken Stock (page 11) or milk

1 cup applesauce

¼ cup walnuts, toasted (page 10)

½ teaspoon dried thyme

½ teaspoon poultry seasoning

½ teaspoon dried rosemary

1 teaspoon Tabasco

Freshly ground black pepper to taste

In a medium skillet, slowly heat the margarine until it melts. Add the apple, onion, celery, and garlic and sauté for 2 minutes. Place the mixture in a large heatproof pan with the bread cubes. Add the hot stock, applesauce, walnuts, thyme, poultry seasoning, rosemary, Tabasco, and black pepper and mix well. Cover the pan with foil and cook for 25 to 30 minutes. Remove the foil and cook for 5 to 10 minutes.

Germany

Herring Salad

**Makes
6 servings**

Matjes are skinned and filleted herring cured in a spicy sweet-and-sour brine.

5 to 6 *matjes* herring fillets

1/2 lemon, sliced

1 red onion, sliced, grilled (see page 9), and cut into 1/2-inch cubes

1 Granny Smith apple, sliced, grilled (page 10), and cut into 1/2-inch cubes

1 cup pickled beets, diced, with 2 tablespoons juice

4 to 6 unpeeled red potatoes, cooked and cut into 1/2-inch cubes

2 tablespoons vegetable oil

4 tablespoons red wine vinegar

4 tablespoons sweet pickle relish or 1 sweet pickle, chopped

2 teaspoons dry mustard

6 lettuce leaves, rinsed and dried

3 hard-boiled eggs, peeled and quartered

1/2 cup sour cream

Place the herring fillets in a nonreactive bowl with 1 cup of cold water and the lemon slices and soak for 25 to 30 minutes. Drain the herring, pat dry, and cut into 1/2-inch pieces. In a medium bowl, combine the herring, onion, apple, beets, and potatoes and mix well.

In a small bowl, combine the vegetable oil, vinegar, relish, and mustard and stir well. Add to the herring mixture, mix well, and marinate for 24 hours in the refrigerator.

To serve, line a dish with the lettuce leaves. Heap the salad in the center, arrange the hard-boiled eggs around the edge, and garnish with sour cream.

Sauerkraut Pie

Buy the best-quality "fresh" sauerkraut, usually found in plastic bags in the refrigerated section of the supermarket. Be sure to rinse and drain the sauerkraut well before combining it with the other ingredients. Serve this dish with your favorite beer.

2 cups sauerkraut, rinsed and drained

2 onions, sliced thin and grilled (page 9)

1 russet potato, peeled and grated

8 cloves Caramelized Garlic (page 8), pureed

2 slices bacon, cooked and chopped fine

1 teaspoon caraway seeds

8 thin slices pumpernickel bread

½ pound bratwurst, grilled (page 10), and sliced ½ inch thick

¼ cup shredded Gruyère cheese

Preheat the grill.

Combine the sauerkraut, onion, potato, garlic, bacon, and caraway seeds in a bowl and mix well. Grease a 9-inch pie plate and line the bottom with the pumpernickle slices. Top with alternating layers of the bratwurst and the sauerkraut mixture. Cover the pan tightly with aluminum foil and grill for 20 minutes with the cover down. Remove the foil, sprinkle evenly with the Gruyère, and return to the grill until the cheese melts, about 5 minutes. Allow the pie to rest for 5 minutes before serving.

Apple Strudel

Use a mixture of slightly tart Granny Smiths and juicy McIntosh apples for this classic dessert. *Strudel* comes from the German word for "whirlpool" or "eddy" and probably refers to the many layers of dough wrapped around the filling.

¼ cup raisins

2 cups coarsely chopped grilled apples (page 10)

2 tablespoons granulated sugar

2 tablespoons brown sugar

Juice and zest from ½ lemon

2 tablespoons brandy

½ teaspoon ground cinnamon

¼ teaspoon ground nutmeg

4 tablespoons cake or cookie crumbs

5 sheets strudel or phyllo dough

¼ cup melted butter or margarine

2 tablespoons sliced almonds (optional)

2 tablespoons melted butter

Cinnamon-sugar

Preheat the grill.

Plump the raisins by soaking them in hot water for 10 minutes. Drain well and pat dry.

Combine the raisins, apple, sugars, lemon juice and zest, brandy, cinnamon, nutmeg, and 2 tablespoons of crumbs in a medium bowl and mix well.

Place a clean kitchen towel on a flat surface. One by one, lay the sheets of strudel dough on top of each other, brushing each layer with the melted butter and a sprinkling of the remaining cake crumbs.

Spoon the apple mixture in a straight line across the top third of the strudel sheet. Starting at the top edge, pull the strudel dough down over the apples and roll it up like a jellyroll. Brush the outside of the strudel with any remaining butter and sprinkle with sliced almonds, if desired. Using two spatulas, carefully transfer the strudel onto a heatproof pan or greased foil. Bake with the grill lid down for 20 to 25 minutes, or until nicely browned. As soon as the strudel is removed, brush it with melted butter and cinnamon-sugar.

Grilled Pretzels

Pretzels are commonly thought to have originated in Bavaria, but they can be traced back to the Romans. Legend says that the crossed ends represent arms folded in prayer. If you like your pretzels crispy, grill them for an additional 5 minutes over very low heat.

2 teaspoons brown sugar

1 teaspoon active dry yeast

3$^1/_2$ cups bread flour or all-purpose flour

$^1/_4$ teaspoon salt

2 cups water combined with 2 tablespoons baking soda

Kosher salt

In a small bowl, combine the sugar and yeast. Add $^1/_4$ cup warm water, mix well, and set aside for 10 minutes.

In a large mixing bowl, combine the flour and salt. Add the yeast mixture and $^3/_4$ cup warm water, and mix until a dough forms, about 2 minutes. Place the dough on a lightly floured surface and knead for 4 to 5 minutes. Place the dough in a lightly greased bowl, cover with a towel, and let rest for 30 minutes.

Cut the dough into four even pieces and flatten each piece. Cut each into 2-by-2-inch pieces, and roll each piece out on a flat surface with the palms of your hands until you have a 6-inch rope. Form the rope into a U and fold the ends over themselves in a pretzel shape.

Place the water-and-baking-soda mixture in a saucepan large enough to dip the pretzels in and bring to a boil. Dip the pretzels into this mixture for 15 seconds, place them on a greased tray, and sprinkle them with Kosher salt. Grill the pretzels for 8 to 10 minutes with the cover down.

Variations:

- Combine ¼ cup grated Parmesan cheese, 1 teaspoon black pepper, and 1 tablespoon grated Cheddar cheese and sprinkle warm pretzels after grilling.
- Sprinkle the pretzels with ½ teaspoon cinnamon before grilling. After grilling, brush them with melted butter and sprinkle them with cinnamon-sugar to taste.
- Mix equal parts cumin and Kosher salt to taste and sprinkle on pretzels before grilling. After grilling, top the pretzels with melted Cheddar cheese, con queso, or salsa.

SCANDINAVIA

Fish and grains have always played a major role in Scandinavian cuisine and appropriately enough our menu begins with a Barley and Buttermilk soup infused with—smoked fish. The Danes love burgers as much as we do, but *frikadeller*, their interpretation of the everyday hamburger, is very much their own. They serve it with a Cheesy Dill Sauce rather than catsup or mustard. Seafood abounds along the coastlines of the North Sea, perfect ingredients for Seafood Sausage which takes on a whole other dimension when finished off over hot coals. And since we should always have our vegetables every day, try a new slant on potatoes called Caramelized Potatoes and an unexpected Creamed Spinach Salad topped with smoked salmon.

Smoked Fish, Barley, and Buttermilk Soup

If you don't have cultured buttermilk on hand, combine 1 cup of heavy cream with 1 tablespoon of lemon juice and set aside for 5 minutes before using.

**Makes
6 servings**

6 cups Chicken Stock (page 11)

½ cup pearl barley

1 onion, sliced, grilled (page 9), and chopped

1 cup smoked fish (trout, eel, whitefish)

1 tablespoon chopped fresh dill

2 bay leaves

1 teaspoon Tabasco

1 cup buttermilk

Freshly ground black pepper to taste

Preheat the grill or side burner.

Combine the chicken stock, barley, and onion in a soup kettle or Dutch oven and bring to a boil. Add half the fish and the dill, bay leaves, and Tabasco, lower the heat, and simmer until the barley is tender, about 45 minutes. Stir in the remaining fish, buttermilk, and black pepper and simmer for 5 minutes. Discard bay leaves before serving.

Frikadeller and Cheesy Dill Sauce

Frikadeller is a Danish version of Salisbury steak or the American hamburger. The next time you pick up a package of ground meat, try this instead of the same old meatballs.

GRILL TEMPERATURE
medium

**Makes
4 servings**

1¹/₂ pounds ground pork or ground beef

1 egg

3 tablespoons bread crumbs

2 tablespoons all-purpose flour

¹/₄ cup milk

1 onion, sliced, grilled (page 9), and chopped

¹/₂ teaspoon ground allspice

Pinch ground nutmeg

Freshly ground black pepper to taste

1 recipe Cheesy Dill Sauce (page 116)

Preheat the grill.

In a medium bowl, combine the pork, egg, bread crumbs, and flour and mix well. Add the milk, onion, allspice, nutmeg, and pepper and blend well. Shape the mixture into eight oval-shaped patties and grill for 3 to 4 minutes on each side.

Scandinavia

Cheesy Dill Sauce

**Makes
1 cup**

½ cup milk

½ cup shredded Swiss cheese

1 tablespoon chopped fresh dill

Heat the milk over low heat. Stir in the cheese and stir until smooth. Stir in the dill.

Seafood Sausage

Seafood sausage is naturally lower in fat than meat sausage. I find it much easier to use cheesecloth instead of sausage casings to shape the sausage. Keep the sausage mixture in the refrigerator while you work with it—it binds better if the ingredients are chilled.

GRILL
TEMPERATURE
medium-low

Makes
4 servings

1 cup heavy cream

1/2 pound lean white fish, such as sole or halibut

1/2 pound salmon fillet

1/2 pound coarsely chopped shrimp or crabmeat

1/4 pound squid, cleaned and chopped

1 onion, grilled (page 9), cooled, and finely chopped

1 whole egg

2 egg whites

1 teaspoon chopped fresh parsley

1/2 teaspoon ground allspice

1/2 teaspoon Tabasco

Pinch ground nutmeg

8 pieces cheesecloth, 6 x 8 inches

Fish Stock (page 12) to cover

Olive oil

1 recipe Sauce for Seafood Sausage (page 119)

Place the cream in the freezer for 15 minutes before mixing the ingredients.

Puree the white fish and salmon in a food processor or meat grinder. Combine the two fish and place in the freezer for 10 minutes.

continued

Scandinavia

117

Fill a large bowl with ice. Place a medium bowl in the center and add the pureed fish, shrimp, squid, onion, egg, egg whites, parsley, allspice, Tabasco, and nutmeg. Add the cream a little at a time, mixing gently.

Wet the cheesecloth and lay on a flat surface. Form ½ cup of the sausage mixture into 1-inch rolls and place on the lower edge of each piece of the cheesecloth. Roll each up and twist the ends of the cheesecloth or secure with string. Refrigerate for 1 hour.

Preheat the grill or side burner.

Pour enough fish stock to cover the seafood sausage into a skillet and bring to a boil. Add the sausage, lower the heat to a simmer, and poach gently for 15 minutes. Remove the sausage and cool. Remove the cheesecloth and brush the sausage with olive oil. Grill the sausage for 3 to 4 minutes, turning once. Serve with sauce.

Variations:

• Substitute ¼ pound smoked salmon for the shrimp.
• Add ¼ pound grilled chopped mushrooms to the fish mixture.

Sauce for Seafood Sausage

2 tablespoons butter

2 tablespoons all-purpose flour

$1/2$ cup chopped grilled red pepper (page 9)

$1/4$ cup chopped grilled onion (page 9)

$1/2$ cup Fish Stock (page 12) or Chicken Stock (page 11)

$1/2$ cup half-and-half

Pinch ground allspice

Pinch ground nutmeg

**Makes
2 cups**

Melt the butter and stir in the flour. Cook over low heat for 1 minute. Add the remaining ingredients and bring to a boil.

Creamed Spinach Salad

Creamed spinach is typically served hot in England, but my version, which is lower in fat than the traditional heavy-cream variety, is best when the chilled dressing is served in warm spinach.

2 pounds fresh spinach, washed and stemmed

1/2 onion, sliced, grilled (page 9), and chopped

6 cloves Caramelized Garlic (page 8), pureed

1/4 cup grated white Swiss cheese

1/4 cup plain yogurt

2 tablespoons low-fat sour cream

1 tablespoon grated Parmesan cheese

1/2 teaspoon Tabasco

Pinch ground nutmeg

Freshly ground black pepper to taste

1 pound salmon fillet

2 tablespoons olive oil

Wash the spinach several times in cool water to remove any grit. Discard stems.

In a small bowl, combine the onion, garlic, Swiss cheese, yogurt, sour cream, Parmesan cheese, Tabasco, nutmeg, and black pepper. Mix well and refrigerate for 1 hour.

Preheat the grill or side burner. Place hickory chips in a smoker box and place on grill. Close cover and smolder for 5 minutes.

Brush the salmon with the olive oil and smoke in closed grill for 7 to 8 minutes.

Toss the spinach with the dressing and place in a serving dish. Top with the smoked salmon and serve.

Caramelized New Potatoes

New potatoes are so sweet they need few ingredients to make a delicious side dish. Here, grilled new potatoes are tossed in a brown glaze spiced with nutmeg.

GRILL TEMPERATURE
medium-high

**Makes
4 servings**

8 medium new potatoes

3 tablespoons butter

2 tablespoons sugar

1 tablespoon chopped fresh parsley

Pinch ground nutmeg

Freshly ground black pepper to taste

Place the potatoes in a medium saucepan, cover with water, bring to a boil, and cook until almost tender, about 15 minutes. Cool slightly and cut in half.

Preheat the grill or side burner.

Heat the butter in a sauté pan, stir in the sugar, and cook until the sugar begins to brown. Add the potatoes, parsley, nutmeg, and pepper and cook, tossing lightly, until the potatoes are heated through and caramelized.

Scandinavia

CANADA

We don't often think of Canada as having a culinary history, yet with its vast open spaces and abundant streams, game is plentiful and the fresh fish is abundant. Much of Canadian food is hearty, making it perfect for grilling. One of my favorite grilled meats is venison—and some of the best comes from Canada. Venison is very lean and tasty, especially when marinated in juniper berries. If there is someone in the crowd who eschews venison, a grilled venison burger will likely fool them into loving it. As for fish and meats, one taste of Hot Smoked Trout or Pork-Sausage and Potato

Casserole, my version of cassoulet, will be enough to convince you that, indeed, food from our good neighbor to the north should not be overlooked. The vegetable dishes here are especially interesting; ordinary vegetables including cauliflower, mushrooms, and rutabagas are transformed with a drizzle of maple syrup, crumbled tangy cheese, or a splash of balsamic vinegar.

Venison Steak

Juniper berries have a rather astringent flavor when raw, but when part of a marinade, they infuse meats with a distinct flavor. If you can't find them, use 2 teaspoons of gin, which is flavored with juniper berries.

GRILL TEMPERATURE
high

Makes
6 servings

1 cup red wine

1 head Caramelized Garlic (page 8), pureed

1 teaspoon dry mustard

1 teaspoon dried rosemary, crushed

3 bay leaves

1 teaspoon dried juniper berries

Six 8-ounce venison round steaks

In a nonreactive bowl, combine the wine, garlic, mustard, rosemary, bay leaves, and juniper berries and mix well. Add the venison steaks and marinate for 24 hours in the refrigerator, turning the steaks several times.

Preheat the grill.

Remove the steaks from the marinade and pat dry. Place the steaks on a hot grill and cook until tender, about 3 to 4 minutes on each side.

Canada

Venison Burgers

GRILL
TEMPERATURE
**high, then
medium**

**Makes
4 servings**

Just like beef, pork, and lamb, certain cuts of venison can be tough. These are the cuts for which quick-cooking burgers, and stews were made.

3 slices bacon, chopped

1 pound ground venison

1 potato, peeled, cooked, and finely diced

¹⁄₂ onion, sliced, grilled (page 9), and chopped

¹⁄₂ head Caramelized Garlic (page 8), pureed

1 egg, lightly beaten

2 tablespoons finely chopped scallions or chives

¹⁄₂ teaspoon dried thyme

Pinch ground nutmeg

1 teaspoon Tabasco

Cook the bacon in a small skillet; drain on a paper towel.

In a medium bowl, combine the bacon, venison, potato, onion, garlic, egg, scallion, thyme, nutmeg, and Tabasco and mix well. Form into 4 patties. Refrigerate the burgers.

Preheat the grill.

Cook the burgers until they are no longer pink in the center, about 4 to 5 minutes on each side, or until the internal temperature is 160°F.

Pork-Sausage and Potato Casserole

GRILL
TEMPERATURE
medium-high

**Makes
4 servings**

Cassoulets are classic French combinations of white beans and various meats. My version features beans as well as potatoes.

2 pounds fresh pork sausage such as bratwurst

2 tablespoons olive oil

1/2 pound sliced bacon, chopped

3 pounds potatoes, peeled and sliced thin

1 cup cooked white beans (navy, Great Northern, cannellini)

2 bay leaves

1 cup chicken stock

1/2 cup heavy cream

Pinch ground nutmeg

Freshly ground black pepper to taste

Preheat the grill.

Brush the pork sausage with the olive oil, place on a medium-hot grill, and cook until the meat is well browned, turning several times.

Arrange the bacon on the bottom of a shallow 3-quart casserole. Alternately layer the pork sausage, potatoes, and beans, slipping the bay leaves in between the layers. Combine the stock, cream, nutmeg, and pepper. Pour the mixture over the meat and potatoes, cover, and cook for 1½ hours with the grill cover down. Discard the bay leaves before serving.

Pork Skewers with Rosemary

GRILL
TEMPERATURE
**high, then
medium-high**

**Makes
4 servings**

I have spent many years in Canada, where the quality of pork is superior. If you can't find rosemary stems, add a teaspoon of dried rosemary to the beer and use metal skewers.

1½ pounds boneless pork sirloin or leg, cut into 2-inch cubes

2 onions, cut into 2-inch wedges

8 rosemary stems

One 12-ounce can beer

1 head Caramelized Garlic (page 8), pureed

Using a metal skewer or sharp knife, pierce a hole in the center of each pork cube and onion wedge. Thread the pork and onion alternately onto the rosemary stems.

Combine the beer and garlic in a shallow dish and marinate the pork skewers for 2 hours in the refrigerator.

Preheat the grill.

Place the pork skewers on the hot grill and sear on all sides for 2 minutes. Move them to the cooler grill edges or reduce the heat to medium and continue cooking for 10 to 12 minutes, basting occasionally with the beer marinade. Do not overcook the pork.

Lamb Chops with Ale

Ale varies in color from light to amber and tends to be sweet, fruity, and smooth. Use an ale that you like to drink in this recipe.

GRILL TEMPERATURE
medium-high

**Makes
6 servings**

1 pint ale

1 head Caramelized Garlic (page 8), pureed

Juice of 2 lemons

2 tablespoons dried rosemary leaves, crumbled

1 tablespoon dried thyme

1 teaspoon Tabasco

Twelve 4-ounce lamb chops

Combine the ale, garlic, lemon juice, rosemary, thyme, and Tabasco. Pour over the lamb and refrigerate for 24 hours.

Preheat the grill.

Remove the chops from the marinade, place them on the grill, and cook for 5 to 6 minutes on each side, basting frequently with the remaining marinade. The lamb is done when the internal temperature is 160°F on an instant-read thermometer.

Canada

129

Charcoal Turkey Steaks

GRILL
TEMPERATURE
**medium-high
charcoal fire**

**Makes
8 servings**

If possible, have your butcher cut the bone-in turkey breast into 1-inch steaks. Otherwise, use boneless turkey breast and cut them yourself. Serve with Grilled Apples.

1 cup apple juice

1 cup fresh cranberries, coarsely chopped

¹⁄₃ cup cider vinegar

1 tablespoon black peppercorns, coarsely crushed

One 8-pound frozen turkey breast, cut into 1-inch steaks

In a shallow bowl, combine the apple juice, cranberries, vinegar, and peppercorns. Add the turkey steaks and spoon the mixture over the pieces so that they are moistened on all sides. Cover and refrigerate for 3 to 4 hours.

Prepare a charcoal fire.

Remove the turkey from the marinade and grill for 7 to 8 minutes on each side, basting occasionally with the remaining marinade.

Grilled Apples

GRILL
TEMPERATURE
high

Makes
2 cups

**2 Granny Smith apples, or other baking variety, halved, cored,
 and brushed with olive oil**

Juice of 1 lime

2 ounces tequila

1 teaspoon fresh cilantro

Freshly ground black pepper

Preheat the grill.

Sear the apples 2 to 3 minutes on all sides and remove. Cut apples into ¼-inch dice and place in a bowl with the lime juice, tequila, cilantro, and black pepper. Mix well.

Canada

Hot Smoked Trout

Canada's rivers run clear and clean, and the trout are plentiful. If a fishing trip to Canada is not in the near future, pick up fresh or frozen, boned and skinned trout fillets at your supermarket or fish store.

½ **cup apple juice**

2 tablespoons olive oil

Juice and zest of 1 lemon

1 tablespoon crushed black peppercorns

1 teaspoon finely chopped fresh parsley

Pinch ground allspice

Two 8-ounce trout fillets, boned and skinned

Combine the apple juice, olive oil, lemon juice and zest, peppercorns, parsley, and allspice in a shallow bowl and mix well. Add the trout and refrigerate for 30 minutes.

Preheat the grill and prepare an iron smoker box with hickory chips.

When the wood is smoldering, grill the fillets for 2 to 3 minutes on each side, with the grill cover down, or until done. The fish will flake easily when cooked.

Cauliflower and Grilled Onion Salad

Even though I like to eat cauliflower raw, I often blanch it, then toss it with grilled onions in a balsamic dressing for a refreshing change.

GRILL TEMPERATURE
medium

**Makes
6 servings**

1 head cauliflower, cut into florets

3 tablespoons olive oil

1 tablespoon balsamic vinegar

4 cloves Caramelized Garlic (page 8), pureed

1 tablespoon coarsely chopped fresh parsley

1 teaspoon coarsely chopped fresh oregano

¹⁄₂ teaspoon Tabasco

Freshly ground black pepper to taste

2 medium red onions, sliced, grilled (page 9), and chopped

Preheat the grill or side burner.

Half fill a 4-quart saucepan with water and bring to a boil. Add the cauliflower and cook for 4 to 5 minutes. Drain well and cool in a serving bowl. Mix the olive oil, vinegar, garlic, parsley, oregano, Tabasco, and pepper in a small bowl. Combine with the cauliflower and onion and toss well. Marinate at room temperature for at least 1 hour before serving.

Canada

Glazed Mushrooms

GRILL
TEMPERATURE
**high, then
medium**

**Makes
4 servings**

You'll be amazed by how much flavor a little cheese gives these smoky grilled mushrooms. Stilton is a variety of blue cheese made in Stilton, England. It has a decidedly Cheddar-like flavor, with the pungency of blue cheese.

1 pound small whole mushrooms

3 tablespoons olive oil

1 onion, grilled (page 9) and chopped

8 cloves Caramelized Garlic (page 8), pureed

¼ cup dry white wine

1 tablespoon coarsely chopped fresh parsley

1 teaspoon Tabasco

Freshly ground black pepper to taste

¼ cup crumbled Stilton or blue cheese

Preheat the grill.

Brush the mushrooms with 2 tablespoons of olive oil and sear on a hot grill until well browned on all sides.

Heat the remaining tablespoon of olive oil in a skillet and sauté the onion and garlic. Add the grilled mushrooms and toss to combine. Add the wine, parsley, Tabasco and pepper. Toss for 1 minute and sprinkle with the cheese. Serve immediately.

Maple-Grilled Rutabaga

Use this maple glaze on other root vegetables—turnips, parsnips, and carrots, even slices of sweet potatoes. As with the rutabagas, these vegetables should first be boiled until almost tender.

GRILL TEMPERATURE
high, then medium

Makes
4 servings

1 medium rutabaga, peeled and cut horizontally into 1-inch slices

¼ cup maple syrup

2 tablespoons melted butter

Pinch ground nutmeg

Freshly ground black pepper to taste

1 teaspoon chopped fresh parsley

Cook the rutabaga in lightly salted water until almost tender. Remove from the pot and drain well.

Combine the syrup, butter, nutmeg, and pepper and mix well. Brush the rutabaga slices with the mixture and set aside for 5 minutes.

Preheat the grill.

Sear the rutabaga slices for 1 minute on each side; move to the cooler edges of the grill or lower the temperature. Cook the rutabaga slices until the centers are tender and the surfaces have caramelized. Remove from the grill and sprinkle with parsley.

Canada

THE UNITED KINGDOM

No one knows for sure how long dishes like Bubble and Squeak, Shepherd's Pie, Irish Stew, and Cock-a-Leekie Soup have been around, but we do know that the people living in the British Isles have been enjoying them for centuries. Now we can experience them on this side of the Atlantic, and preparing them outdoors on the grill makes them even more exciting.

They may have a reputation for a strictly meat and potatoes cuisine, but the cooks in the U.K. know how to prepare vegetables creatively, too. From "tinned" corn to an array of carrot dishes as well as salads, we've taken the best of them and gussied them up on the grill.

Wings for the Queen

A generous dose of strong English stout, gooey honey, and zesty mustard give these wings a tangy flavor—a refreshing change from those that blister your mouth. Enjoy with your favorite ale.

12 chicken wings

1 pint stout

3 bay leaves

1 tablespoon honey

1 teaspoon dry mustard

1 teaspoon black peppercorns, crushed

Cut and discard the bony wing tips. Cut each wing in half.

Combine the stout, bay leaves, honey, dry mustard, and peppercorns in a resealable plastic bag. Add the wings, seal the bag, and shake until the wings are completely covered with the marinade. Refrigerate for 2 hours, turning the bag occasionally.

Preheat the grill.

Remove the wings from the marinade and place them on the grill. Turn the wings after 4 to 5 minutes, baste with the marinade, and cook them until tender, 10 to 15 minutes longer, basting occasionally.

Cock-a-Leekie Soup

GRILL
TEMPERATURE
**high, then
medium**

**Makes
6 servings**

This hearty chicken soup is a Scottish favorite, with oatmeal or barley added instead of rice or noodles. The name is a slurring of the chief ingredients, chicken and leeks.

One 3-pound chicken, cut into 8 pieces

¼ cup Poultry Rub (page 140)

2 slices bacon, chopped, or ¼ cup chopped ham

2 leeks, whites parts only, grilled (page 9) and chopped

1 onion, sliced, grilled (page 9), and chopped

2 ribs celery, sliced

4 cloves garlic, sliced

6 cups Chicken Stock (page 11)

3 bay leaves

1 teaspoon Tabasco

1 teaspoon chopped fresh parsley

½ teaspoon dried thyme

½ cup pearl barley, cooked according to package directions

Preheat the grill.

Season the chicken with the Poultry Rub and sear on all sides over high heat until well browned. Cook the bacon in a large stockpot or Dutch oven until light brown. Add the leek, onion, celery, and garlic and cook for 2 minutes, stirring constantly. Add the chicken pieces, chicken stock, bay leaves, Tabasco, parsley, and thyme. Bring to a boil, lower the heat, and simmer for 30 minutes. Add the cooked barley and cook until heated through. Discard the bay leaves. Remove the chicken from the bones and return the meat to the soup.

**The United
Kingdom**

Poultry Rub

Makes
about ½ cup

2 tablespoons sweet paprika

2 tablespoons brown sugar

1 tablespoon dried rosemary, crumbled

1 tablespoon dried parsley

1 tablespoon garlic powder

1 teaspoon dried sage

¼ teaspoon ground nutmeg

Combine all of the ingredients in a small bowl and mix well. Store in a tightly covered jar.

Ham and Bean Soup

GRILL
TEMPERATURE
medium-high,
then medium

Makes
6 servings

Traditionally made from leftovers, soups were probably the original one-dish suppers. This is loosely based on a French soup called *garbure*, which is a combination of several leftover soups.

2 tablespoons olive oil

1 ham steak, grilled (page 10) and chopped

1 onion, sliced, grilled (page 9), and chopped

½ cup chopped carrot

½ cup diced celery

6 cloves Caramelized Garlic (page 8), pureed

6 cups Chicken Stock (page 11)

1 potato, peeled and diced

6 plum tomatoes, grilled (page 9) and chopped

1 tablespoon cider vinegar

1 tablespoon chopped fresh parsley

1 teaspoon dried thyme

1 teaspoon dried rosemary

1 teaspoon Tabasco

2 bay leaves

Freshly ground black pepper to taste

One 16-ounce can white beans (Great Northern or cannellini), rinsed and drained

Preheat the grill or side burner.

Heat the olive oil in a large stockpot or Dutch oven and sauté the ham, onion, carrot, celery, and garlic for 3 to 4 minutes. Add the chicken stock, potato, tomato, vinegar, parsley, thyme, rosemary, Tabasco, bay leaves, and pepper. Bring the soup to a boil, lower the heat, and simmer for 45 minutes. Stir in the beans and simmer for 15 minutes. Discard the bay leaves before serving.

Grilled Ham, Cheese, and Pasta (Macaroni and Cheese)

GRILL TEMPERATURE

medium-high, then low

Makes 6 servings

Macaroni and cheese is simple to make, but we're so used to taking it out of the box or the freezer that we've forgotten how good it tastes when made from scratch. Use good-quality sharp cheeses.

2 tablespoons butter or margarine

One 8-ounce ham steak, grilled (page 10) and chopped

1 onion, sliced, grilled (page 9), and chopped

8 cloves Caramelized Garlic (page 8), pureed

2 tablespoons all-purpose flour

4 cups Chicken Stock (page 11) or vegetable stock

2 bay leaves

1/2 teaspoon dried thyme

1/2 teaspoon Tabasco

Pinch ground nutmeg

2 cups heavy cream or half-and-half

1 cup shredded sharp Cheddar cheese

1/2 cup shredded Swiss cheese

2 tablespoons grated Parmesan cheese

1 1/2 pounds uncooked elbow pasta, shells, or other small pasta

1 recipe Mac Topping (optional; recipe follows)

Preheat the grill or side burner.

Melt the butter in a large stockpot or saucepan. Add the ham, onion, and garlic and sauté for 1 minute. Add the flour and cook for 1 to 2 minutes, stirring constantly. Slowly add the stock, and bring to a boil. Lower the heat, add the bay leaves, thyme, Tabasco, and nutmeg, and simmer for 10 minutes.

Stir in the cream and heat to a simmer. Slowly add the Cheddar, Swiss, and Parmesan cheeses, stirring until they melt and the sauce is smooth. Stir in the cooked pasta. Place in a serving dish and eat immediately or sprinkle with the Mac Topping, lower the lid, and grill for 5 minutes..

Variations:

- Add 1/2 cup cooked green peas with the pasta.
- Add 1/2 cup grilled sliced mushrooms with the pasta.
- Served topped with grilled tomatoes.

Mac Topping

4 tablespoons (1/2 stick) butter or margarine, melted

6 tablespoons bread crumbs

1 thick slice onion, grilled (page 9) and chopped

1 tablespoon chopped fresh herbs, such as parsley, cilantro, basil, sage, or chives

Freshly ground black pepper to taste

Place all of the ingredients in a medium bowl and mix well.

GRILL
TEMPERATURE
medium

Makes
6 servings

The United
Kingdom

Bubble and Squeak

GRILL
TEMPERATURE
medium-high,
high for ham
steak

Makes
6 servings

The unusual name of this English dish comes from the sound the ingredients supposedly make while the dish is cooking. Since this dish was designed to use up Sunday's leftovers, any kind of grilled meat can be substituted for the ham. If using game or beef steak, serve the dish with Horseradish-Mustard Sauce (page 146).

2 tablespoons butter or margarine

1 onion, sliced, grilled (page 9), and chopped

1 head Caramelized Garlic (page 8), pureed

1 leek, white part only, split, grilled (page 9), and chopped

1 cup sliced cooked carrots

3 cups coarsely chopped cabbage

1 teaspoon dried thyme

1 teaspoon Tabasco

Pinch ground nutmeg

Freshly ground black pepper to taste

3 whole cooked russet potatoes

2 tablespoons olive oil

Sweet paprika

One 12-ounce ham steak

Preheat the side burner.

Melt the butter in a large saucepan. Add the onion, garlic, and leek and sauté for 2 minutes. Add the carrots and cook until the vegetables become slightly brown. Add the cabbage, thyme, Tabasco, nutmeg, and pepper and cook for 8 to 10 minutes.

While the cabbage is cooking, cut the potatoes horizontally into ½-inch slices, brush with olive oil, and sprinkle with paprika. Grill the slices, turning once, until they're nicely brown.

Quickly grill the ham steak 4 to 5 minutes on both sides over high heat. Cut the ham steak into pieces and serve with the cabbage and potato slices.

Horseradish-Mustard Sauce

**GRILL
TEMPERATURE**
medium

**Makes
2 cups**

Typically you would add water to dry English mustard to use it as a dip. I got the idea of using beer from an English waitress who worked with me for many years.

> **1 cup beer**
>
> **2 tablespoons dry English mustard**
>
> **¼ cup honey**
>
> **1 cup plain yogurt**
>
> **1 tablespoon chopped chives**
>
> **2 tablespoons drained horseradish**

Preheat the grill or side burner.

Combine the beer, mustard, and honey in a saucepan. Bring to a boil, remove from the heat, and cool. Slowly whisk in the yogurt. Stir in the chives and horseradish and mix well. Chill for 1 hour before serving.

Irish Stew

GRILL
TEMPERATURE
high, then low

**Makes
6 servings**

Balsamic vinegar was probably never added to stewpots in Ireland, but I think it gives my Irish stew a delicate sweetness. Make this a day in advance to let the flavors develop.

2 pounds lamb stew meat, cut into 1½-inch pieces

4 tablespoons olive oil

1 onion, sliced, grilled (page 9), and chopped

1 rib celery, chopped

1 carrot, diced

6 cloves Caramelized Garlic (page 8), pureed

1 tablespoon dried rosemary

2 tablespoons balsamic vinegar

4 cups Chicken Stock (page 11)

2 cups sliced new red potatoes

2 bay leaves

Preheat the grill.

Toss the stew meat with 2 tablespoons of olive oil. Place on a hot grill and sear on all sides until well browned, 5 to 6 minutes.

Heat the remaining olive oil in a large soup kettle or stockpot and sauté the onion, celery, carrot, and garlic for 1 to 2 minutes. Add the lamb, rosemary, and vinegar and cook for 2 minutes. Add the chicken stock, potatoes, and bay leaves. Bring to a boil, lower the heat, and simmer until the lamb is tender, about 1 hour. Discard the bay leaves before serving.

Shepherd's Pie

GRILL
TEMPERATURE
high, then
medium-high

Makes
6 servings

Shepherd's pie was created by the Scottish as a way to stretch Sunday's roast into Monday's supper. Traditionally, the meat and vegetables are covered with mashed potatoes before baking, but this version uses thinly sliced potatoes instead.

1 pound ground beef

½ pound ground lamb

½ pound mushrooms, grilled (page 9) and chopped

2 onions, sliced, grilled (page 9), and chopped

2 carrots, chopped

1 rib celery, chopped

½ cup fresh or frozen green peas

6 cloves Caramelized Garlic (page 8), pureed

1 teaspoon ground thyme

1 teaspoon fresh chopped parsley

1 teaspoon Tabasco

Pinch ground nutmeg

Freshly ground black pepper to taste

1 cup hot Chicken Stock (page 11)

3 russet potatoes, peeled and sliced very thin, or 2 cups seasoned
    mashed potatoes

Olive oil

Mix the ground beef and lamb and form ten patties.

Preheat the grill.

Place the patties on the hot grill and sear until brown on both sides, 4 to 5 minutes total cooking time, turning once. Place the patties, mushroom, onion, carrot, celery, peas, garlic, thyme, parsley, Tabasco, nutmeg, and pepper in a large shallow casserole and mix well. Pour the hot stock over the meat and vegetables. Cover with the thinly sliced potatoes. Brush the potatoes with olive oil and place the casserole on the grill. Lower the grill lid and cook for 30 minutes.

Charred Stuffed Trout

GRILL
TEMPERATURE
**high, then
medium**

**Makes
4 servings**

I prepared this dish for friends I was visiting in England, where trout is abundant. This is a great company dish.

One 8-ounce salmon fillet

$1/2$ cup bread crumbs from day-old French or Italian bread

2 tablespoons mayonnaise

1 teaspoon chopped fresh dill

$1/2$ teaspoon Tabasco

Freshly ground black pepper to taste

3 egg whites

6 large shrimp, peeled, deveined, and coarsely chopped

Four 12-ounce trout, cleaned, gutted, and boned

2 tablespoons olive oil

Preheat the grill.

Process the salmon in a food processor using the on/off button until it is ground but not pureed. Add the bread crumbs, mayonnaise, dill, Tabasco, and pepper and blend for 30 seconds. Add the egg whites and mix for 1 minute. Fold in the shrimp with a rubber spatula.

Fill each trout with a quarter of the stuffing. Secure with skewer or toothpick. Brush the trout with the olive oil and grill for 2 minutes on each side. Lower the heat to medium or move the trout to the cooler edges of the grill and cook for 3 to 4 minutes.

Glazed Carrots

GRILL
TEMPERATURE
medium

**Makes
6 servings**

This recipe is my version of Vichy carrots—a dish traditionally made with the mineral water from that region of France (but you can use your favorite home-town sparkling mineral water). To make fast work of this dish, buy prepeeled baby carrots in your supermarket.

1 pound Belgian or baby carrots, about 2 inches long, peeled

2 tablespoons butter

1 onion, sliced, grilled (page 9), and chopped

2 tablespoons honey

1 cup club soda or carbonated mineral water

Pinch ground nutmeg

Freshly ground black pepper to taste

1 tablespoon chopped fresh Italian parsley

Preheat the grill or side burner.

Parboil the carrots in lightly salted water for 3 minutes. Drain well.

Heat a sauté pan and melt the butter. Add the onion and cook until light brown. Add the carrots and honey and cook for 2 to 3 minutes. Add the club soda a little at a time and cook for 4 to 5 minutes, until the water has evaporated and the carrots are tender. Season with the nutmeg, pepper, and parsley and toss well.

Sherried Carrots

GRILL
TEMPERATURE
medium

**Makes
6 servings**

Carrots are prepared in a myriad of ways in England; they seem to show up at every meal. I always have them on hand and like to prepare them with a little sherry and brown sugar.

2 cups Belgian or baby carrots, peeled

2 tablespoons butter

1 rib celery, chopped to the size of the carrots

1 leek, white part only, well cleaned, chopped to the size of the carrots

2 tablespoons brown sugar

Pinch ground cinnamon

2 ounces sherry or other sweet wine or rum

Freshly ground black pepper to taste

Preheat the grill or side burner.

Cook the carrots in lightly salted water until they are almost tender, about 8 minutes.

Melt the butter in a sauté pan and add the celery and leek. Cook for 1 minute, add carrots, sugar, and cinnamon, and cook 4 to 5 minutes, or until the carrots are tender. Stir in the sherry and season with black pepper.

Tinned Corn Salad

What Americans call canned corn is referred to as "tinned corn" in other English-speaking countries. Here corn is tossed in a dressing that combines sweet, acid, and spicy flavors with cooling mint.

6 ears of fresh corn, grilled (page 8), or two 12-ounce cans kernel corn

1 red bell pepper, grilled (page 8) and chopped

3 Italian frying peppers, grilled (page 8) and chopped

1 head Caramelized Garlic (page 8), pureed

1 red onion, sliced, grilled (page 9), and chopped

2 tablespoons olive oil

Juice and zest of 1 lemon

2 tablespoons honey

1 teaspoon Tabasco

2 tablespoons chopped fresh mint

Freshly ground black pepper to taste

Lettuce leaves

Preheat the grill.

Remove the grilled kernels from the corn cobs and combine with the peppers, garlic, onion, olive oil, lemon juice and zest, honey, Tabasco, mint, and black pepper. Toss gently.

Line a serving dish with lettuce leaves and pile the salad in the center.

**The United
Kingdom**

Grilled Cucumbers with Dill

GRILL
TEMPERATURE
high

**Makes
6 servings**

I find it hard to pass up cucumbers when the price is right, but I get tired of using them in salads. Try cucumbers as a cooked vegetable for a refreshing change.

4 cucumbers, peeled, halved, and seeded

2 tablespoons olive oil

2 onions, sliced and grilled (page 9) slowly so they caramelize

3 cloves Caramelized Garlic (page 8), pureed

¹/₂ cup plain yogurt

¹/₂ cup sour cream

2 tablespoons cider vinegar

2 tablespoons coarsely chopped fresh dill

¹/₂ teaspoon Tabasco

Freshly ground black pepper to taste

1 red bell pepper, grilled (page 8) and cut into thin strips

Preheat the grill.

Brush the cucumbers with olive oil, place them on a very hot grill, and sear them on all sides. When the cucumbers are cool enough to handle, cut them into thin strips, place them in a medium bowl, and gently mix in the caramelized onion and garlic. Fold in the yogurt, sour cream, vinegar, dill, Tabasco, and black pepper. Marinate in the refrigerator for at least 1 hour or overnight. Line a serving dish with lettuce leaves and pile the cucumber mixture on top. Garnish with red-pepper strips.

Grilled Celery Hearts

Most grocery stores sell hearts of celery in plastic bags. If you can't find them, cut off the lower 4 inches of celery bunches and use the remaining celery in salads or as crudités.

¼ cup cider vinegar

2 tablespoons sugar

2 whole celery hearts

2 tablespoons olive oil

Freshly ground black pepper to taste

Preheat the grill or side burner.

Bring 2 cups of water to a boil in a medium saucepan. Add the vinegar and sugar and boil for 3 to 4 minutes. Add the celery, lower the heat, and cook for 5 minutes. Remove the celery and drain well. Split the celery hearts, brush them with the olive oil, and grill it for 2 minutes on each side. Sprinkle with black pepper.

GRILL
TEMPERATURE

high, then low;
high for grilling

Makes
4 servings

The United
Kingdom

Mushroom Salad

This unusual dish goes well with grilled Belgian endive and crusty French bread.

One 10-ounce package button mushrooms

1 cup fresh shiitake mushrooms, stems removed

2 Portobello mushroom caps

1/4 cup olive oil

2 heads Caramelized Garlic (page 8), pureed

1 cup shallots (about 4 to 5) or 1 onion, grilled (page 9) until caramelized

Juice of 2 lemons

1 teaspoon coarsely chopped fresh mint

1/2 teaspoon dried thyme

1/2 teaspoon dried rosemary

1 teaspoon Tabasco

Preheat the grill.

Brush the mushrooms with 2 tablespoons of olive oil, place on a very hot grill, and sear on all sides. Leave the button mushrooms whole, but slice the shiitake and Portobello caps and mix them together in a serving bowl. Add the garlic, shallots, remaining olive oil, lemon juice, mint, thyme, rosemary, and Tabasco and mix well. Marinate the mushrooms for 1 hour before serving.

Zucchini Stuffed with Corn Ratatouille

GRILL
TEMPERATURE
medium

**Makes
6 servings**

Here is proof that you don't have to be a vegetarian to appreciate the virtues of vegetables. This mélange of summer vegetables can be served as a first course or as a side dish served alongside grilled fish or steak.

2 medium zucchini

1 small eggplant, peeled, sliced, and grilled (page 8)

Kernels from 2 ears grilled corn (page 8), or 1 cup canned or frozen corn kernels

1 red bell pepper, grilled (page 8) and chopped

½ red onion, sliced, grilled (page 9), and chopped

3 plum tomatoes, grilled (page 9) and chopped

5 to 6 cloves Caramelized Garlic (page 8), pureed

½ teaspoon dried thyme

½ teaspoon dried rosemary

1 teaspoon Tabasco

Freshly ground black pepper to taste

2 tablespoons olive oil

Preheat the grill.

Cut the zucchini diagonally into ¾-inch slices and grill on one side. Scrape out the flesh of the grilled side, leaving a nest. Place the scrapings in a bowl with the eggplant, corn, red pepper, onion, tomatoes, garlic, thyme, rosemary, Tabasco, and black pepper. Stuff the nests with the vegetable mixture and drizzle with olive oil. Grill for 10 to 12 minutes.

**The United
Kingdom**

Individual Yorkshire Puddings

GRILL
TEMPERATURE

**medium, then
medium-low**

**Makes
8 to 10 servings**

Yorkshire pudding comes from Yorkshire county in northern England, and no beef roast in that country is complete without one. To test for doneness, tap the outside; it should sound hollow.

1½ cups all-purpose flour

1½ cups milk

3 eggs

4 ounces (1 stick) butter, melted

Freshly ground black pepper to taste

Pinch ground nutmeg

8 to 10 tablespoons vegetable oil or meat drippings

Place the flour in a medium bowl. Combine ½ cup of the milk and the eggs and beat well. Make a well in the center of the flour and pour in the mixture, whisking constantly. Slowly add the remaining milk, whisking constantly, until the mixture is smooth. Stir in the melted butter, pepper, and nutmeg. Refrigerate for 15 minutes.

Preheat the grill.

Place a tablespoon of vegetable oil in the bottom of eight to ten 2½-inch muffin cups. Place the muffin cups on the grill, close the cover, and heat for 2 minutes on medium. Stir the batter and fill the muffin cups to within ¼ inch of the top. Place the filled muffin cups on the grill, close the cover, and heat for 8 minutes on medium; reduce the temperature to medium-low and bake for 2 minutes.

MEXICO, CENTRAL AND LATIN AMERICA, AND THE CARIBBEAN

So many of the foods we consider to be truly American or European orginated in Latin America. Tomatoes, all types of peppers, chocolate, pineapple, peanuts, vanilla, turkey, corn, pumpkin, sweet potatoes, and squash are all part of our diet today—thanks to explorers who picked them up along the way on their voyage to the New World.

The fare south of the border is distinctive yet simple—much of it was originally cooked out of doors over an open fire. In this chapter you'll find recipes for Barbecue Burrito, Empanadas, and Tamales—all adapted for cooking on the grill. Wait until you smell the smoky aromas from the chilies, cumin, and oregano that are found in many of these Mexican dishes.

From the lush Caribbean islands there are grilled Bermudian-Style Pork Chops rubbed with a fragrant sweet and spicy mixture and Cuban Stew, a humble dish of rice and beans that gets an elegant lift from the addition of chicken and chorizo sausage.

Fill the air with the multilayered aromas of Smoked Vegetable Soup where the vegetables are given a totally new dimension by grilling them first. Make Posole for your next large gathering. You can prepare it in advance, then top the festivities off with Sopaipillas for dessert. Bring on the mariachi band and strike up the music.

Poblano Chili Linguine

GRILL
TEMPERATURE
medium

Makes
4 servings

Fresh poblano chilies are greenish-black in color, 4 to 5 inches long, and 2 to 3 inches wide. Their flavor varies from mild to slightly hot. Once they have been dried, they are called ancho chilies. The best poblanos are found in central Mexico, but they are also grown in the American Southwest.

6 poblano chilies

1 red bell pepper

1 head Caramelized Garlic (page 8), pureed

½ onion, sliced, grilled (page 9), and chopped

¼ cup chopped fresh cilantro

Juice of 2 limes

½ cup olive oil

2 tablespoons pecans or walnuts, toasted on grill (page 10)

1 pound linguine, cooked

Freshly ground black pepper to taste

Preheat the grill.

Grill the chilies and red pepper, turning occasionally, until they're charred on all sides. Remove and set aside. When cool enough to handle, remove the skins and seeds. Cut the bell pepper into long strips.

Place the chilies, garlic, onion, cilantro, and lime juice in a blender and process for 30 seconds. Add the olive oil and process for 30 seconds. Add the toasted nuts and strips of red pepper and stir well. Toss with the hot linguine, sprinkle with black pepper, and serve.

Mexico, Central
and Latin America,
and the Caribbean

Smoked Vegetable Soup

Smoking vegetables gives them an extra layer of flavor that is reminiscent of crispy fried bacon. Enjoy the flavor without all of the fat in this healthy vegetable soup.

**Makes
6 servings**

4 ears fresh corn

1 onion, sliced

8 plum tomatoes, cut in half through the stem ends

1 leek, white part only, cleaned

3 tablespoons olive oil

1 rib celery, diced

1 carrot, peeled and diced

6 cloves Caramelized Garlic (page 8), pureed

8 cups vegetable or chicken broth

1 cup peeled and diced yellow turnip or sweet potato

3 bay leaves

1 tablespoon chopped fresh parsley

Freshly ground black pepper to taste

Preheat the grill and place an iron smoker box filled with hickory inside.

Pull back the corn husks, remove the silk, and reposition the husks. Soak the ears for 20 minutes in water to cover.

Place the wet ears of corn on the grill. Brush the onion, tomatoes, and leek with 2 tablespoons of the olive oil and sear for 5 minutes on the grill, with the grill lid down, turning once. Remove the vegetables, but leave the corn on the grill to smoke for 15 minutes longer. Remove the corn, let it cool slightly, and cut off the kernels.

Heat the remaining tablespoon of olive oil in a stockpot or soup kettle. Add the onion, celery, carrot, and garlic, and sauté for 5 minutes. Add the stock, tomatoes, corn, turnip, bay leaves, and parsley and bring to a boil. Lower the heat and simmer for 45 minutes. Season with black pepper. Discard the bay leaves before serving.

Barbecue Burrito

Makes
6 servings

Here's a good example of Know Your Fire. Don't be afraid to experiment. I began with a Southern-style American barbecue sauce with chicken and replaced the bun with a Mexican flour tortilla.

1½ **pounds boneless and skinless chicken legs and thighs**
½ **pound boneless and skinless chicken breasts**
¼ **cup Barbecue Burrito Rub (recipe follows)**
2 **cups Barbecue Burrito Sauce (page 166)**
Twelve 10-inch flour tortillas

Season the chicken parts with the Barbecue Burrito Rub and refrigerate for 1 hour.

Preheat the grill.

Sear the chicken on a hot grill for 2 minutes on each side. Move the chicken to the cooler grill edges or lower the heat to medium, and cook until tender, 4 to 5 minutes longer. Remove the chicken from the grill and cool for 5 minutes. Shred the chicken meat, combine it with the barbecue sauce in a small saucepan, and simmer for 20 to 30 minutes on the grill or side burner.

To serve, place 3 to 4 tablespoons of the chicken mixture in the center of each flour tortilla. Fold each side toward the center and roll up from the bottom. Place the burritos on a medium-hot grill and heat on both sides for a total of 1 to 2 minutes.

Barbecue Burrito Rub

1 tablespoon sweet paprika

1 tablespoon dried oregano

1 tablespoon black pepper

1 tablespoon garlic powder

1 tablespoon lemon zest

1 tablespoon ground cumin

**Makes
about ⅓ cup**

Combine all of the ingredients in a small bowl and mix well.

Store in a tightly covered jar.

Barbecue Burrito Sauce

The simple addition of cumin transforms this sauce from the Carolinas to the Yucatán.

2 tablespoons olive oil

1 onion, sliced, grilled (page 9), and chopped

1 green bell pepper and 1 red bell pepper, grilled (page 8) and chopped

1 head Caramelized Garlic (page 8), pureed

¼ cup chopped scallion

½ cup cider vinegar

½ cup brown sugar

1 cup tomato puree

1 teaspoon dried thyme

1 teaspoon dried oregano

1 teaspoon dried cumin

1 teaspoon Tabasco

Preheat the grill or side burner.

Heat the olive oil in a medium saucepan. Add the onion, peppers, garlic, and scallion and cook over high heat for 2 to 3 minutes. Add the vinegar and brown sugar and boil until the liquid is reduced by half. Stir in the tomato puree, thyme, oregano, cumin, and Tabasco and simmer the sauce for 5 minutes over low heat.

Empanadas

GRILL
TEMPERATURE
medium-low

**Makes
6 servings**

Spanish for "baked in pastry," small hand-held empanadas can be made with a variety of fillings ranging from meat and vegetables to fruit. Use leftovers for the filling.

3 cups all-purpose flour

¼ teaspoon salt

¼ cup (½ stick) margarine or butter, cut into small pieces

½ pound chopped beef, browned

½ pound chorizo sausage, grilled (page 10) and chopped

4 plum tomatoes, grilled (page 9) and chopped

2 tablespoons chopped scallion

4 cloves Caramelized Garlic (page 8), pureed

1 tablespoon coarsely chopped fresh cilantro

1 teaspoon curry powder

1 teaspoon Tabasco

Olive oil

Combine the flour and salt in a medium bowl. Cut in the margarine until the mixture resembles cornmeal. Add ¾ cup of water, a little at a time, working the dough until it begins to hold together. Knead the dough briefly until it's pliable. Cover the dough and set it aside for 1 hour.

To make the filling, combine the cooked chopped beef, chorizo, tomato, scallion, garlic, cilantro, curry powder, and Tabasco in a medium bowl and mix well.

continued

Roll the dough out ¼ inch thick on a lightly floured surface and cut into 4-inch circles with a cookie cutter. Place a teaspoon of filling in the center of each circle, moisten the edges with water, and fold in half, forming a half-moon-shaped turnover. Brush with olive oil and place on the grill for 3 to 4 minutes on each side.

Tamales

GRILL
TEMPERATURE
medium-high

**Makes
6 servings**

You can make your own cornhusks by drying fresh cornhusks in the sun or in the oven on very low heat. Trim the ends so that they're flat with squared ends.

**18 cornhusks, banana leaves, or pieces of aluminum or
   8 x 8-inch parchment paper**

Tamale Mix

3 cups fine yellow cornmeal or masa harina

½ cup margarine

6 cloves Caramelized Garlic (page 8), pureed

2 teaspoons ground cumin

1 teaspoon baking powder

1 teaspoon Tabasco

Pinch ground nutmeg

Pinch black pepper

3½ cups hot Chicken Stock (page 11)

1 recipe tamale filling (pages 170–171)

If using corn husks, soak them in hot water for 1½ hours.

In a large bowl, mix the cornmeal, margarine, garlic, cumin, baking powder, Tabasco, nutmeg, and pepper until well blended. Add the chicken stock and stir the mixture until it becomes a smooth paste. Mix with a wooden spoon.

Drain the husks and pat them dry. Spread 3 to 4 tablespoons of the cornmeal mixture across the center of each husk, and place one of the fillings given below on top.

Fold the bottom of the husk up over the filling and fold the top portion down. Fold both ends over each other at the center and tie with strips of husk or with string.

Preheat the grill or side burner.

Place a large stockpot of boiling water on the grill or side burner. Put the tamales in a strainer over the boiling water, cover tightly, and steam for 30 minutes.

Following are a variety of tamale fillings.

continued

Chicken Tamale Filling

1¹/₂ pounds skinless and boneless chicken legs and thighs

3 tablespoons Barbecue Burrito Rub (page 165)

2 cups Barbecue Burrito Sauce (page 166)

Season the chicken with the Barbecue Burrito Rub and refrigerate for 1 hour.

Preheat the grill.

Sear the chicken for 2 minutes on each side over high heat. Move it to the cooler edges of the grill or lower the heat to medium and cook until tender, 4 to 5 minutes. Remove the chicken from the grill and cool for 5 minutes. Shred the chicken, combine it with the Barbecue Burrito Sauce, and simmer for 20 to 30 minutes over medium heat. Use 2 tablespoons of the chicken mixture for each tamale.

Shrimp Tamale Filling

1¹/₂ pounds large shrimp, peeled and deveined

1 tablespoon olive oil

2 cups Barbecue Burrito Sauce (page 166)

Brush the shrimp with the olive oil and sear on the grill for 2 minutes on each side. Remove and coarsely chop. In a medium saucepan combine the shrimp with the Barbecue Burrito Sauce and cook for 5 minutes over low heat.

Pork Tamale Filling

1½ pounds pork shoulder, cut into 1-inch cubes

3 tablespoons olive oil

1 teaspoon Tabasco

1 teaspoon chopped fresh cilantro

2 tablespoons Caribbean Dry Rub (page 175)

1 onion, sliced, grilled (page 9), and chopped

½ cup diced celery

1 head Caramelized Garlic (page 8), pureed

½ cup tomato puree

1½ cups Chicken Stock (page 11)

2 tablespoons red wine

GRILL TEMPERATURE

high, then low

Combine the pork cubes with 1 tablespoon of the olive oil, Tabasco, cilantro, and Caribbean Dry Rub and mix well. Place the meat on a very hot grill and sear on all sides for 5 to 6 minutes. Heat the remaining olive oil in a medium stockpot and sauté the onion, celery, and garlic, stirring occasionally. Add the meat and tomato puree and cook two minutes. Add the chicken stock and wine, lower the temperature and simmer until the meat is tender, about 1 to 1½ hours. Use 2 tablespoons of the pork mixture for each tamale.

Tamale Pie

Every country has its own version of meat pies. In Mexico, a hot and spicy beef mixture is covered with a crunchy cornmeal topping, not unlike tamales, which consist of savory or sweet fillings wrapped in *masa* dough, then coddled in a corn husk.

1 pound skirt steak

¼ cup Tamale Beef Rub (recipe follows)

2 cups tomato sauce (commercial or homemade)

1 cup corn kernels, from grilled corn (page 8) or canned

1 onion, sliced, grilled (page 9), and chopped

6 cloves Caramelized Garlic (page 8), pureed

2 jalapeño peppers, grilled (page 8), seeded, and chopped

1 tablespoon coarsely chopped fresh cilantro

1 teaspoon ground cumin

1 teaspoon Tabasco

Cornmeal Topping

2 cups cornmeal

1 cup milk

2 tablespoons butter, melted

1 tablespoon sugar

½ teaspoon salt

1 teaspoon coarsely cracked black pepper

1 cup grated Monterey Jack cheese

Rub the steak with the Tamale Beef Rub and refrigerate for 1 hour.

Preheat the grill.

Grill the steak for 2 minutes on each side over high heat. Cool slightly and slice into thin strips across the grain. In a medium bowl, combine the meat, tomato sauce, corn, onion, garlic, jalapeños, cilantro, cumin, and Tabasco and mix.

To make the cornmeal topping, combine the cornmeal, 1 cup of water, milk, butter, sugar, pepper, and salt.

Place a layer of meat mixture in a 10- or 12-inch pie dish. Top with half of the cheese. Repeat the layers. Spread the cornmeal topping evenly over the cheese and bake for 30 to 35 minutes over medium heat with the cover down.

Tamale Beef Rub

1 tablespoon ground cumin

1 tablespoon ground coriander

1 teaspoon garlic powder

1 teaspoon ground allspice

1 teaspoon ground nutmeg

1 teaspoon coarsely ground black pepper

½ teaspoon cayenne

½ teaspoon dry mustard

Combine all of the ingredients in a small bowl and mix well. Store in a tightly covered jar.

Bermudian-Style Pork Chops

Toss out that bottled barbecue sauce—all you need to flavor these pork chops is my Caribbean Dry Rub, a sweet, spicy mixture made with ingredients you have in your cupboard.

**Makes
4 servings**

Four 8-ounce center-cut pork chops

$^1/_2$ cup Caribbean Dry Rub (recipe follows)

4 tablespoons olive oil

1 red Bermuda onion

2 tomatoes, thickly sliced

1 large green bell pepper, seeded and cut into 4 pieces

4 cloves Caramelized Garlic (page 8), pureed

1 recipe Grilled Tomato Rice (page 176)

Rub the pork chops with the Caribbean Dry Rub and refrigerate for 24 hours.

Preheat the grill.

Shake off any excess rub from the pork chops and brush them with 2 tablespoons of olive oil. Sear the chops until well browned, about 3 to 4 minutes on each side. Remove the chops from the grill, place them in a baking pan, and return the pan to the grill.

Meanwhile, brush the vegetables with the remaining olive oil and grill over medium-high heat until tender. Spread each chop with Caramelized Garlic and top with 2 slices of grilled onion, 2 slices of tomato, and a piece of green pepper.

Serve with Grilled Tomato Rice.

Caribbean Dry Rub

¼ cup brown sugar

1 tablespoon sweet paprika

1 tablespoon ground cumin

1 teaspoon garlic powder

1 teaspoon freshly ground black pepper

1 teaspoon ground coriander

1 teaspoon ground allspice

Makes
½ cup

Combine all of the ingredients in a small bowl and mix well. Store in a tightly covered jar.

Grilled Tomato Rice

GRILL
TEMPERATURE
**high, then
low**

**Makes
4 servings**

Plain rice may not be the most interesting food, but add tomatoes and seasonings to it and it is transformed.

1 cup rice

8 plum tomatoes, grilled (page 9), and chopped

1 onion, sliced, grilled (page 9), and chopped

8 cloves Caramelized Garlic (page 8), pureed

2 teaspoons fennel seeds

2 cups Chicken Stock (page 11) or vegetable stock

2 scallions, chopped

½ teaspoon Tabasco

Preheat the grill or side burner.

Combine the rice, tomato, onion, garlic, and fennel seeds in a medium saucepan and cook for 2 minutes, stirring constantly. Add the stock, scallion, and Tabasco. Bring to a boil, lower the heat, cover the pan, and simmer until the rice is tender, 15 to 20 minutes.

Chili Pork Chops

I travel around the United States to appear on local and national TV shows and to give cooking demonstrations. Whenever I shop for ingredients, I always look in the produce aisle, first and primarily for the selection of chilies. Fresh chilies are a great way to wake up those taste buds.

2 jalapeño or serrano chilies, chopped

6 cloves Caramelized Garlic (page 8), pureed

2 tablespoons sugar

1 teaspoon dried thyme

1 teaspoon dried rosemary

1 teaspoon sweet paprika

Four 8-ounce loin pork chops

2 tablespoons olive oil

Combine the chilies, garlic, sugar, thyme, rosemary, and paprika and mix well. Rub the mixture onto both sides of the pork chops and refrigerate for 1 hour.

Preheat the grill.

Brush the chops with the olive oil, place on a hot grill, and cook for 4 to 5 minutes on each side; lower the heat to medium and cook until desired doneness, about 10 to 12 minutes on each side, depending on thickness.

GRILL TEMPERATURE
high, then medium

Makes 4 servings

Mexico, Central and Latin America, and the Caribbean

Posole

Traditionally served at Christmastime in Mexico's Pacific Coast region, *posole* is a thick soup made with hominy—dried corn with the hull and germ removed. For a quicker version of *posole*, use shoulder pork chops, which require only 2 hours of marinating time and 2 hours of smoking. For an even speedier version, chop a grilled ham steak and add it to the hominy.

One 4-pound pork butt or shoulder
2 tablespoons Tabasco
½ cup Posole Pork Rub (recipe follows)
2 tablespoons olive oil
1 onion, sliced, grilled (page 9), and chopped
1 head Caramelized Garlic (page 8), pureed
4 cups hot Chicken Stock (page 11) or water
4 cups canned drained hominy
1 tablespoon coarsely chopped fresh cilantro

Brush the pork on all sides with the Tabasco, rub with the Posole Pork Rub, and refrigerate for 24 hours.

Prepare a smoker or grill to cook slowly for 8 to 10 hours, using chunks of mesquite. Smoke the pork until it pulls away from the bone, between 8 and 9 hours. Remove the pork from the smoker and let it rest for 1 hour before shredding the meat and discarding the bone.

In a large stockpot or soup kettle, heat the olive oil and cook the pork, onion, and garlic for 2 minutes. Add the hot stock and hominy and simmer for 30 minutes. Stir in the cilantro and serve.

Posole Pork Rub

2 tablespoons brown sugar

1 tablespoon ground cumin

1 tablespoon black pepper

1 tablespoon garlic powder

1 tablespoon sweet paprika

1 tablespoon dried thyme

1/2 teaspoon ground nutmeg

1/2 teaspoon ground allspice

**Makes
about 1/2 cup**

Combine all of the ingredients in a small bowl and mix well. Store in a tightly sealed container.

Cuban Stew

Although I've never visited Cuba, I feel as though I'm there whenever I stay in Miami, where the Cuban influence is rich and plentiful. Originally cooked in a large clay pot over an open fire, this stew is chock-full of chicken and sausage.

**Makes
4 servings**

One 2½- to 3-pound chicken, cut into 8 to 10 pieces

4 tablespoons olive oil

½ pound chorizo sausage, grilled (page 10)

1 onion, sliced, grilled (page 9), and chopped

1 head Caramelized Garlic (page 8), pureed

2 teaspoons ground cumin

**2 teaspoons ground saffron or turmeric (use turmeric for color
  if expense is a consideration)**

1 teaspoon Tabasco

4 cups Chicken Stock (page 11)

6 plum tomatoes, grilled (page 9) and chopped

1 cup canned red kidney beans, rinsed and drained well

1 cup rice

Freshly ground black pepper to taste

Preheat the grill.

Brush the chicken with 2 tablespoons of olive oil and quickly sear over high heat for 2 to 3 minutes on all sides. Heat the remaining 2 tablespoons of olive oil in a large stockpot or soup kettle. Add the chicken, chorizo, onion, garlic, cumin, turmeric, and Tabasco and cook, stirring constantly, for 4 to 5 minutes.

Add the stock, tomatoes, and beans and cook for 1 hour over medium-low heat. Add the rice and cook for 20 minutes. Season with black pepper and serve.

Salsa Chicken

Salsa is the Mexican word for "sauce." Some salsas are cooked and some are raw, some are hot, others are mild, but to my mind, all salsas should be made with the freshest ingredients available.

GRILL TEMPERATURE
medium, then low

Makes
4 servings

Juice of 2 lemons

1 head Caramelized Garlic (page 8), pureed

2 tablespoons light soy sauce

2 teaspoons freshly ground black pepper

Two 2½-pound chickens, split in half lengthwise

2 cups Salsa for Chicken (page 182)

Combine the lemon juice, garlic, soy sauce, and pepper in a bowl and mix well. Brush the chicken with the marinade and refrigerate for 1 hour.

Preheat the grill.

Remove the chicken from the marinade and grill, skin side down, for 8 to 10 minutes over medium heat. Turn, and cook the chicken 8 to 10 minutes longer. Move the chicken to the cooler edges of the grill or reduce the heat to low and continue cooking until the chicken is done, a total of 25 to 30 minutes. Serve with Salsa for Chicken.

Salsa for Chicken

Makes
2 cups

Make your salsa and refrigerate it for a day to really improve the flavor.

1 onion, sliced, grilled (page 9), and coarsely chopped

6 plum tomatoes, grilled (page 9) and chopped

2 green bell peppers, grilled (page 8) and chopped

Juice of 2 limes

1/2 head Caramelized Garlic (page 8), pureed

2 tablespoons raisins

2 tablespoons chopped almonds

1 tablespoon coarsely chopped fresh cilantro

Combine all of the ingredients, mix well, and set aside for 30 minutes before serving.

Smoked Chicken Enchiladas

Enchilada, literally translated, means "chilied up." Whether rolled, folded, or stacked, enchiladas lend themselves to all kinds of fillings. For a change, try turkey or duck instead of the chicken.

PREPARE A SMOKER FOR
6 HOURS (CONSULT
MANUFACTURER'S
INSTRUCTIONS)

GRILL
TEMPERATURE
medium

Makes
4 servings

Two 2½-pound chickens, split in half lengthwise

½ cup Smoked Chicken Dry Rub (page 184)

Vegetable trimmings for smoker

Eight 6-inch corn or flour tortillas

Olive oil

2 cups tomato sauce (commercial or homemade)

2 crushed dried chilies, or more to taste

1 tablespoon coarsely chopped fresh cilantro

1 teaspoon ground cumin

1 teaspoon dried oregano

1 teaspoon Tabasco

¼ cup sliced black olives

2 scallions, chopped

1 cup shredded sharp Cheddar cheese

Rub the chickens with the Smoked Chicken Dry Rub and refrigerate for 2 hours.

Prepare the water smoker, adding trimmings from onions, celery, carrots, or other vegetables to the smoker's water container. When the coals turn to white ash, place the chickens on the racks, and smoke at 200 to 205°F for 2½ hours.

continued

(Ducks will require 3 hours of smoking and turkeys from 4 to 6 hours, depending on their size and outside temperature.) Remove the chickens when they're done, and let them rest for 30 minutes. Remove the meat from the bones.

Place 2 tablespoons of chicken in the center of each tortilla and roll up. Brush with olive oil and grill for 2 minutes on each side. Arrange in a single layer in a casserole.

In a medium bowl, combine the tomato sauce, chilies, cilantro, cumin, oregano, and Tabasco and pour over the tortillas. Scatter the olives and scallion over the top and place the casserole on the grill for 10 minutes with the grill cover down. Sprinkle with the cheese and cook for 10 minutes longer with the top down.

Smoked Chicken Dry Rub

Makes almost ½ cup

¼ cup sugar

1 teaspoon cayenne

1 teaspoon sweet paprika

1 teaspoon chili powder

1 teaspoon garlic powder

1 teaspoon ground coriander

1 teaspoon dried thyme

1 teaspoon dried rosemary, crumbled

Combine all of the ingredients in a small bowl and mix well. Store in a tightly sealed container.

Shrimp with Garlic and Plantains

GRILL TEMPERATURE
high, then medium

Makes
6 servings

Shrimp are classified according to size, and you will find that a pound of large shrimp has 26 to 30. Here they are cooked Latin American-style, with seared plantains. You've probably seen plantains in the supermarket; they look like large bananas and are sometimes called "cooking bananas." A plantain is ripe when it turns dark, almost black. Serve the dish with Grilled Pineapple and Lentils (page 187).

2 tablespoons olive oil

Juice of 2 limes

1 head Caramelized Garlic (page 8), pureed

1 teaspoon Tabasco

1 pound large shrimp, peeled and deveined

3 medium ripe and juicy plantains

2 tablespoons olive oil

2 tablespoons butter

2 tablespoons sugar

1 tablespoon honey

Combine the olive oil, lime juice, garlic, and Tabasco in a medium bowl and mix well. Add the shrimp, toss gently, and refrigerate for 30 minutes.

Preheat the grill.

continued

Place the shrimp on skewers and grill for 5 to 6 minutes on each side, or until opaque.

Peel the plantains and slice them ¼-inch thick on an angle. Brush with the olive oil, sear on both sides, lower heat, and cook until tender, about 3 to 4 minutes total. Melt the butter in a sauté pan. Add the sugar and cook, stirring constantly, until the sugar caramelizes. Take care not to burn the sugar. Add the grilled plantains and honey and toss lightly. Serve with the grilled shrimp.

Grilled Pineapple and Lentils

Though native to Central and South America, nowadays pineapples are also grown in Hawaii. Grilling them caramelizes pineapples' natural sugars, making them a delicious, sweet counterpoint to the soothing lentils.

GRILL TEMPERATURE
medium-high

Makes
6 servings

1 cup lentils

2 tablespoons olive oil

1 onion, sliced and grilled (page 9)

1 rib celery, chopped

3 cloves Caramelized Garlic (page 8) pureed

2 to 3 cups Chicken Stock (page 11) or vegetable stock

1 small, very ripe pineapple, peeled, sliced, and grilled (page 10), or 1 cup canned chunks with juice

1 tablespoon chopped fresh cilantro

1 teaspoon Tabasco

Preheat the grill or side burner.

Wash the lentils in cool water and remove any twigs or pebbles. Drain well. Heat the olive oil in a stockpot, add the lentils, onion, celery, and garlic, and cook for 2 to 3 minutes, stirring constantly. Add 2 cups stock, the pineapple, cilantro, and Tabasco and simmer until the lentils are tender, about 1 hour. Add the remaining stock if the lentils are too thick.

Mexico, Central and Latin America, and the Caribbean

Red Pepper Relish

Sweet, hot, and a snap to prepare, this relish will keep for several days in the refrigerator.

6 plum tomatoes, grilled (page 9) and chopped

¹/₂ cup cider vinegar

2 tablespoons sugar

2 tablespoons raisins

2 red bell peppers, grilled (page 8) and diced

1 onion, sliced, grilled (page 9), and chopped

2 jalapeño peppers, grilled (page 8), seeded, and diced

Preheat the grill or side burner.

In a small saucepan, combine the tomatoes, vinegar, sugar, and raisins. Bring to a boil, lower the heat, and simmer until half the liquid has evaporated. Cool slightly and add the bell peppers, onion, and jalapeños. Refrigerate for 1 hour before using.

Black Bean and Onion Relish

GRILL
TEMPERATURE
medium

**Makes
4 servings**

If you can't smell the aroma of a spice when you remove the cover, it's time to replace it. Cumin gives this easy-to-make relish a distinct flavor. Use it on grilled burgers or full-flavored fish.

¼ cup cider vinegar

4 tablespoons sugar

1 teaspoon cumin seeds

2 onions, sliced, grilled (page 9), and finely chopped

6 cloves Caramelized Garlic (page 8), pureed

1 tablespoon coarsely chopped fresh cilantro

½ teaspoon Tabasco

One 16-ounce can black beans, rinsed and well drained

Preheat the grill.

Combine the vinegar, sugar, and cumin seeds in a small saucepan. Bring to a boil and reduce the liquid by half. Add the onion, garlic, cilantro, and Tabasco and mix well. Add the beans and toss lightly.

Plantains with Garlic and Vinegar

Once plantains, or *plátanos*, were found only in Caribbean, Latin American, and Mexican markets, but now most supermarkets stock them. Caribbean cooks use them when they are green and starchy, but Mexican cooks prefer them very ripe and juicy.

Use fully ripe plantains for this recipe so the sweetness will balance the acidity of the vinegar.

2 ripe plantains

4 tablespoons olive oil

¼ cup cider vinegar

Juice of 1 lemon

2 heads Caramelized Garlic (page 8), pureed

1 finely chopped serrano or jalapeño chili

1 tablespoon chopped fresh cilantro

Freshly ground black pepper to taste

Preheat the grill.

Peel the plantains, cut them ¼ inch thick on an angle, and brush them with the olive oil.

Combine the vinegar, lemon juice, garlic, and chili in a small saucepan. Bring to a boil and reduce the liquid by half.

Quickly sear the plantains on both sides on a hot grill. Remove and arrange on a serving dish. Pour the vinegar sauce over the top and sprinkle with the cilantro and black pepper.

Sopaipillas

FRYING
TEMPERATURE
370°F

**Makes
3 dozen**

These Mexican deep-fried pastry puffs are drizzled with honey and served warm. Although you can heat the oil on the side burner outdoors, the *sopaipillas* can also be cooked in an electric fryer indoors.

3 cups all-purpose flour

2¹/₂ teaspoons baking powder

1 tablespoon sugar

1 teaspoon salt

2¹/₂ tablespoons margarine

1 cup less 1 tablespoon lukewarm water

2 cups oil for frying

Honey

In a medium bowl, combine the flour, baking powder, sugar, and salt. Cut in the margarine until the mixture resembles coarse meal. Add the water, a few tablespoons at a time, stirring with a fork until the mixture almost cleans the sides of the bowl. Knead the dough until pliable. Cover and let it rest for 1 hour.

Roll out the dough ¹/₄ inch thick on a lightly floured surface and cut into 3-inch rounds. Heat the oil to 370°F. Add the *sopaipillas*, a few at a time, and turn them immediately. As soon as they begin to brown, turn them again. Remove, drain well on paper towels, and while still warm, drizzle with honey.

THE MIDDLE EAST

This chapter essentially presents you with a Middle Eastern menu. Chunks of lamb are marinated, skewered, and grilled and then served with a wonderful onion sauce. The aroma alone will bring people flocking to the grill.

Serve them with Middle Eastern favorites like Grilled Moussaka, Greek Stuffed Peppers, and Grilled Eggplant with Toasted Pine Nuts. Make sure to prepare enough of the Imam Flat Bread, a pizza with a Middle Eastern twist and one that lends itself perfectly to the grill.

Imam Flat Bread

Imam is Turkish for "priest." Legend has it that a holy man gained immortality when he swooned over the eggplant topping on this pizza.

1 small eggplant, peeled, grilled (page 8), and sliced

4 plum tomatoes, grilled (page 9) and chopped

½ onion, sliced, grilled (page 9), and chopped

8 cloves Caramelized Garlic (page 8), pureed

2 tablespoons raisins

1 teaspoon ground allspice

½ teaspoon dried thyme

¼ teaspoon ground cinnamon

Pinch ground nutmeg

Freshly ground black pepper to taste

4 tablespoons olive oil

**Two 8-ounce portions pizza dough from a basic cookbook or
    frozen or refrigerated pizza dough**

Preheat the grill.

Combine the eggplant, tomato, onion, garlic, raisins, allspice, thyme, cinnamon, nutmeg, and pepper in a medium bowl and stir in 2 tablespoons of olive oil.

Using your fingertips, spread each portion of pizza dough ½ inch thick. Place the dough in two 9-inch pie pans and let it rest for 5 minutes. Brush the dough on both sides with olive oil and grill for 4 to 5 minutes, or until grill marks appear. Remove the pizzas from the grill, brush the tops with oil, turn them over, and top the grilled sides evenly with the eggplant mixture. Return the pizzas to the grill, close the cover, and cook until the pizzas are fully baked, 5 to 7 minutes. Drizzle with any remaining olive oil before serving.

Grilled Moussaka

GRILL TEMPERATURE

high for grilling
meat patties;
medium-high for
grilling eggplant
and potatoes;
low for
simmering sauce;
medium for
baking casserole

Makes
6 servings

This Greek specialty is a wonderful company dish because it can be prepared a day in advance and tastes even better when reheated. Choose ground lamb, beef, or pork to make the patties. To make a vegetarian moussaka, leave out the meat.

1 pound lean ground lamb, pork, or beef

3 tablespoons butter

$\frac{1}{2}$ onion, sliced, grilled (page 9), and chopped

5 cloves Caramelized Garlic (page 8), pureed

3 tablespoons all-purpose flour

2 cups half-and-half

$\frac{1}{2}$ cup crumbled feta cheese

$\frac{1}{4}$ cup grated Parmesan cheese

$\frac{1}{4}$ cup raisins, plumped for 10 minutes in $\frac{1}{2}$ cup boiling water

2 tablespoons pine nuts or sliced almonds

1 teaspoon dried thyme

1 teaspoon Tabasco

$\frac{1}{2}$ teaspoon dried rosemary, crushed

Pinch ground nutmeg

2 eggplants, peeled, sliced, and grilled (page 8)

2 russet potatoes, peeled, sliced $\frac{1}{4}$-inch thick, and grilled (page 9) or boiled

2 tablespoons olive oil

Preheat the grill.

Form the ground meat into 8 small, thin patties and grill over high heat until no longer pink in the center. When cool, break each patty into several chunks.

Melt the butter in a medium saucepan on the grill or side burner. Add the onion and garlic and cook for 1 minute. Stir in the flour and cook for 2 minutes, stirring constantly. Slowly whisk in the half-and-half, lower the heat, and simmer the sauce for 3 to 4 minutes. Add the feta, Parmesan, raisins, pine nuts, thyme, Tabasco, rosemary, and nutmeg and mix well.

Spread a thin layer of sauce in a greased 3-quart casserole; cover with half the eggplant, meat patties, and sauce. Repeat the layers.

Top with a layer of sliced potatoes and drizzle with the olive oil. Cover the pan tightly with aluminum foil and bake in a covered grill for 20 minutes. Remove the foil, lower the grill cover, and cook for an additional 10 minutes. Remove the casserole and let it sit for 10 minutes before serving.

Lamb on Skewers

GRILL TEMPERATURE
high, them medium

If you choose to use the less expensive lamb shoulder, double the marinating time.

Makes 4 servings

1½ pounds lamb from the leg, loin, or shoulder

2 cups Curry Marinade (recipe follows)

2 green bell peppers, seeded and cut into 1-inch squares

1 onion, cut into 1-inch pieces

2 zucchini or yellow squash, cut into 1-inch pieces

1 ripe pineapple, peeled and cut into 1-inch cubes

1 cup Onion Sauce (page 200)

Marinate the lamb in the Curry Marinade for 1 hour, refrigerated. Arrange the lamb, pepper, onion, squash, and pineapple on skewers.

Preheat the grill.

Place the skewers on the hot grill for 2 minutes, turning them so they sear on all sides. Move them to the cooler edges, or lower the temperature to medium, and cook for 5 to 6 minutes on each side. Total cooking time is 10 to 12 minutes.

Boil the marinade in a separate saucepan until it thickens, and use it to baste the lamb while it's cooking. Serve with the Onion Sauce.

Curry Marinade

Curry powder is not a single spice, but rather a mixture of several spices. These generally include coriander, ginger, pepper, paprika, and turmeric, but the blend differs from region to region, and the number of different spices can be as many as twenty.

When buying curry powder, or any spice, always buy the highest quality you can find. Old or inexpensive curry powder can ruin the dish.

Makes about 1¼ cups

1 cup pineapple juice

2 tablespoons balsamic vinegar

6 cloves Caramelized Garlic (page 8), pureed

1 tablespoon curry powder

1 teaspoon Tabasco

Pinch ground cinnamon

Combine all of the ingredients in a small bowl and mix well.

Onion Sauce

The sweeter the onion, the sweeter the sauce. Caramelizing the onion brings out its natural sweetness and removes a good part of the acid.

½ cup plain yogurt

½ cup mayonnaise

½ onion, sliced, grilled (page 9), and chopped

3 cloves Caramelized Garlic (page 8), pureed

1 tablespoon coarsely chopped fresh mint

Juice of 1 lemon

1 teaspoon Tabasco

Freshly ground black pepper to taste

Combine all of the ingredients in a small bowl, mix well, and refrigerate for 1 hour before serving.

Greek Stuffed Peppers

Serve these at room temperature for the best flavor. They make an unusual first course.

GRILL
TEMPERATURE
high

Makes
6 servings

6 medium bell peppers

1 cucumber, peeled, seeded, and chopped

1 red onion, sliced, grilled (page 9), and chopped

3 plum tomatoes, grilled (page 9) and chopped

¹/₄ cup crumbled feta cheese

¹/₄ cup olive oil

1 head Caramelized Garlic (page 8), pureed

3 tablespoons pine nuts

2 tablespoons cider vinegar

1 teaspoon chopped fresh rosemary

1 teaspoon chopped fresh oregano

¹/₂ teaspoon Tabasco

Freshly ground black pepper to taste

Preheat the grill.

Lightly char the peppers for 5 to 6 minutes on a hot grill, turning them every 2 minutes. When the peppers are cool enough to handle, carefully cut out the stems and remove the seeds, taking care to keep the peppers intact.

In a separate bowl, combine the remaining ingredients and mix well. Stuff the peppers with the mixture and refrigerate for 2 hours. Serve at room temperature.

Grilled Eggplant with Toasted Pine Nuts

GRILL TEMPERATURE
high

**Makes
6 servings**

Toasting pine nuts deepens their flavor, making them strong enough to stand up to the assertive flavor of smoky eggplant. Store any extra nuts in the refrigerator for up to 3 months, or in the freezer for up to 9 months.

2 medium eggplants, peeled and sliced ¼ inch thick

¼ cup olive oil

1 medium onion, sliced, grilled (page 9), and chopped

1 head Caramelized Garlic (page 8), pureed

3 tablespoons pine nuts

Juice of 2 lemons

1 tablespoon chopped fresh mint

Pinch ground cinnamon

Pinch ground allspice

½ teaspoon Tabasco

Lettuce leaves, washed and dried

Preheat the grill.

Brush the eggplant slices with half of the olive oil. Place the slices on a hot grill and cook until they're nicely brown and the interiors are tender. Remove the slices from the grill, cool, cut into 2- to 3-inch pieces, and place in a deep bowl with the onion and garlic.

Place the pine nuts in a pan on the grill, and cook until they turn light brown, shaking the pan frequently.

Combine the remaining olive oil, lemon juice, mint, cinnamon, allspice, and Tabasco and mix well. Pour the mixture over the eggplant, marinate for 2 hours at room temperature, and drain off any liquid. To serve, spread the lettuce leaves on a serving platter, top with the eggplant, and sprinkle with the toasted pine nuts.

PACIFIC RIM

Pacific Rim countries are those with shorelines that touch the Pacific Ocean, extending from China and Japan down to Australia. The cuisines of these countries have frequently been adapted to fit into the American menu. Now we take the dishes a step further and cook them on the grill, using American staples found in any supermarket.

These recipes offer a new and exciting approach to entertaining, from the Chinese-inspired Vegetable Spring Rolls and prize-winning Turkey-and-Black-Bean Wontons to the Japanese Pork Spare Ribs Teriyaki and Australian Carpetbag Steak.

Barbecue Steamed Pork Buns

GRILL
TEMPERATURE
high

Makes
8 servings

Dim sum are China's favorite snack food and Steamed Pork Buns made with a sweet yeast dough is one of their favorites. Enjoy them any time of the day with a steaming cup of Chinese tea.

1 cup milk, at 90°F

$1/2$ cup sugar

$3/4$ ounce fresh yeast

4 cups all-purpose flour

2 tablespoons vegetable oil or solid white shortening

Pinch salt

Meat or Vegetarian Filling (see Note)

1 cup cooked smoked or grilled pork, chicken, or vegetables, chopped

$1/4$ cup catsup

2 tablespoons honey

2 tablespoons light soy sauce

1 teaspoon sesame oil

Combine the milk, sugar, and yeast in a small bowl, mix well, and set aside for 15 to 20 minutes. In a large bowl combine the flour, shortening, and salt. Pour the liquid ingredients into the dry ingredients and mix well. Place the mixture on a flat surface and knead until smooth, about 5 to 7 minutes. Place the dough in a greased bowl, cover, and set aside until the dough doubles in volume, about 1 hour. Fold the dough over itself and let rest another 20 minutes.

Combine all the filling ingredients and mix well.

To Prepare Buns: Pinch off a piece of dough the size of a walnut and flatten it into a 3-inch circle between the palms of your hands. Place a spoonful of filling in the center and gather up the edges loosely around the filling. Twist the edges closed and set aside, twisted side down, for 15 minutes on a 3-inch square of wax paper or parchment paper for each bun.

Place the pork buns on bamboo steamer racks. Fill a wok with 2 to 3 inches of water and bring to a boil over a hot grill. Stack up to three steamer racks, cover, and place in the wok. Steam the buns 30 to 45 minutes

Note: 1/2 cup hoisin sauce can be substituted for the catsup, honey, soy sauce, and sesame oil.

Vegetable Spring Rolls

Traditionally served on the first day of the Chinese New Year, these small stuffed pastries are filled with both raw and cooked vegetables, giving them an unusual texture.

2 small bok choy, white stalks grilled (page 8) and shredded,
leaves shredded (about 2 cups)
1 cup shiitake mushrooms, grilled (page 9) and chopped
1/2 onion, sliced very thin and grilled (page 9)
2 cups finely shredded savoy cabbage
1 small carrot, cut into 2-inch julienne strips
1 head Caramelized Garlic (page 8), pureed
One 2-inch piece fresh ginger, peeled (page 8) and chopped
2 tablespoons light soy sauce
1 scallion, chopped
1 teaspoon sesame oil
1 package (20 to 25) spring roll skins
Vegetable oil for frying
1 1/2 cups Peanut Sauce (page 210)

Place the grilled bok choy, mushrooms, and onion in a colander and drain well. The filling should be cool and as dry as possible. Combine with the cabbage, carrot, garlic, ginger, soy sauce, scallion, and sesame oil in a medium bowl and mix well.

While working with the spring-roll skins, cover the unused ones with plastic wrap to prevent them from drying out. Lay a spring-roll skin on a flat surface with a corner of the skin facing you; place 2 tablespoons of filling in the center. Brush the inside of the top edge with water. Fold the left and right corners over the filling, and roll up the skin away from you. Press the top edge firmly to seal.

Preheat the grill or side burner.

Pour vegetable oil into a deep skillet to a depth of 1 inch and heat to 360°F. Fry the spring rolls, a few at a time, for 3 to 4 minutes, or until golden brown. Serve with peanut sauce.

To grill the spring rolls, brush the outsides with vegetable oil and grill on medium-low heat about 8 minutes.

Peanut Sauce

**Makes
1 cup**

Great sauces and dips like this one can be made with ingredients you have stored in your pantry.

½ **cup chunky peanut butter, at room temperature**

½ **cup pineapple juice**

4 cloves Caramelized Garlic (page 8), pureed

1 tablespoon light soy sauce

1 teaspoon hot chili oil or Tabasco

1 teaspoon peeled and chopped fresh ginger

1 teaspoon sesame oil

Blend the peanut butter and pineapple juice until smooth. Add the garlic, soy sauce, chili oil, ginger, and sesame oil and mix well. Set aside for 30 minutes before serving.

Turkey-and-Black-Bean Wontons

GRILL
TEMPERATURE
medium

Makes
4 servings

I put this recipe together at the last minute to serve at a Hunger Benefit party, where, to my surprise, all of the food was going to be entered in a competition. My Chinese-inspired dish took first place.

8 to 10 ounces ground turkey

1/2 cup cooked black beans

1/2 onion, sliced, grilled (page 9), and chopped

8 cloves Caramelized Garlic (page 8), pureed

1 scallion, chopped

1 tablespoon soy sauce

1 tablespoon fresh ginger, grilled (page 8) and chopped

1 teaspoon sesame oil

One 12-ounce package wonton wrappers

Vegetable oil for deep frying

1 recipe Wonton Dipping Sauce (page 213)

In a medium bowl, combine the chopped turkey, black beans, onion, garlic, scallion, soy sauce, ginger, and sesame oil and mix well. Refrigerate the mixture for 1 hour.

Lay out five to six wontons at a time on a flat surface with one of the corners directly in front of you. Place a teaspoon of the chicken mixture in the center of each wonton wrapper and brush the edges lightly with water. Fold the top corner over the filling to make a triangle and press the edges to seal. Moisten the two side points with water, overlap them firmly, and seal.

Continue making the wontons until the filling is used up. Keep the wonton wrappers and stuffed wontons covered with plastic wrap to prevent them from drying out. Refrigerate if not cooked immediately.

Preheat the grill or side burner.

Fill a small, deep pot half full with vegetable oil and heat to 360°F. Add the wontons, a few at a time, and fry until they are light brown on both sides, turning once. They will cook very rapidly. Repeat until the wontons are all cooked. Serve warm with Wonton Dipping Sauce.

The wontons can also be steamed for 8 to 10 minutes or grilled. To grill the wontons, steam them first, coat them lightly with olive oil, and grill for 2 minutes.

Wonton Dipping Sauce

1/2 cup hoisin sauce

1/4 cup catsup

4 cloves Caramelized Garlic (page 8), pureed

2 tablespoons light soy sauce

1 tablespoon sesame oil

1 scallion, chopped

One 1-inch piece fresh ginger, peeled, sliced, and grilled (page 8)

1/2 teaspoon hot chili oil or Tabasco

Combine all of the ingredients in a small bowl and mix well. Set aside for 30 minutes before serving.

Grilled Vegetarian Lo Mein

Before stir-frying, make sure all the ingredients are close at hand. Once you start to cook, the ingredients are added within seconds of each other, leaving no time to stop and chop.

2 tablespoons peanut or vegetable oil

1 onion, sliced, grilled (page 9), and chopped

2 scallions, white parts chopped, green parts cut into 1-inch pieces

6 cloves Caramelized Garlic (page 8), pureed

2 tablespoons fresh ginger, peeled, sliced, and grilled (page 8)

1 small bok choy, white stems sliced thin, greens coarsely chopped

1 red bell pepper, grilled (page 8) and chopped

1 Chinese eggplant, cut into long, thin strips

6 shiitake mushrooms, grilled (page 9) and sliced

1 pound lo mein noodles, cooked

1 cup Chicken Stock (page 11)

2 tablespoons light soy sauce

1 teaspoon sesame oil

2 scallions, chopped, for garnish

Preheat the grill or side burner.

Heat the peanut oil in a wok or a pan with a wide bottom on the grill or side burner. Add the onion, scallion, garlic, and ginger and stir-fry for 30 seconds. Add the bok choy, red pepper, eggplant, and mushrooms and stir-fry for 10 seconds. Stir in the cooked noodles, chicken stock, soy sauce, and sesame oil and cook for 1 minute. Sprinkle scallions on top and serve immediately.

Carpetbag Steak

GRILL
TEMPERATURE
medium-high

Makes
4 servings

Legend says that this steak was named for carpetbags filled with luxury items that the wealthy carried with them when they traveled. Some believe it's Australian in origin, others claim it's pure American.

2 pounds flank, rump, or sirloin steak

1/2 pound shrimp, peeled and deveined, or 1 cup shucked oysters

1/2 cup corn kernels, from grilled corn on the cob or canned

1/4 cup bread crumbs

3 tablespoons olive oil

6 cloves Caramelized Garlic (page 8), pureed

1 tablespoon coarsely chopped fresh cilantro

Freshly ground black pepper to taste

Preheat the grill.

If using flank steak, butterfly the meat, pound it evenly, and cut it into four equal pieces. If using rump or sirloin steak, cut a pocket in the side.

Combine the remaining ingredients in a medium bowl and mix well. If using the flank steak, place equal amounts of stuffing on each piece, roll up, and secure with a small skewer or toothpick. If using the rump or sirloin steak, fill the pocket with the stuffing and secure with a small skewer or toothpicks.

Grill the steaks for 4 to 5 minutes on each side, or until the desired doneness is attained. Remove the toothpicks or skewers before serving.

Pork Spare Ribs Teriyaki

St. Louis, Kansas City, and Texas come to mind when we think of barbecued ribs but the Japanese have been barbecuing for centuries. My daughter Dori created this version of Japanese-style ribs. The secret to their flavor is the slow cooking.

1/2 cup light soy sauce

1/4 cup dry sherry

8 cloves Caramelized Garlic (page 8), pureed

2 tablespoons honey

2 scallions, chopped

1 tablespoon chopped fresh ginger

2 pounds pork spare ribs

In a small bowl, combine the soy sauce, sherry, garlic, honey, scallion, and ginger and mix well. Pour the mixture over the ribs and refrigerate for several hours, turning occasionally.

Preheat the grill.

Place the ribs on the grill and cook slowly, basting occasionally with the marinade. The cooking time should be about 1½ hours or until a fork, inserted between the bones, slides in easily.

Sweet-and-Sour Chicken

Boiling sugar and vinegar together produces a balanced sweet-and-pungent flavoring just as pronounced as any seasoning you can buy. Sweet-and-sour seasoning is used in Chinese, German, and Sicilian cooking.

1¹⁄₂ pounds boneless and skinless chicken cutlets, cut into 1-inch strips

2 tablespoons vegetable oil

Several long strips fresh ginger (about 2 tablespoons), grilled (page 8)

2 tablespoons cider vinegar

2 tablespoons brown sugar

1 tablespoon light soy sauce

1 tablespoon catsup

1 teaspoon sesame oil

¹⁄₂ fresh pineapple, grilled (page 10) and cubed

1 red bell pepper, grilled (page 8) and cut into 1-inch squares

1 green bell pepper, grilled (page 8) and cut into 1-inch squares

1 onion, sliced, grilled (page 9), and coarsely chopped

2 scallions, cut on an angle into 2-inch pieces

Preheat the grill.

Brush the chicken strips with the oil and sear on all sides on the grill for 2 to 3 minutes, removing them just before they're fully cooked.

Heat a wok or saucepan over high heat on the grill or side burner. Add the ginger, vinegar, brown sugar, soy sauce, catsup, and sesame oil. Bring to a boil and cook for 2 minutes. Toss in the pineapple, peppers, onion, and scallion and mix well. Add the chicken strips and cook until done, about 1 minute.

Sweet-and-Sour Fish

GRILL
TEMPERATURE
medium-high

**Makes
2 servings**

I based this recipe on a fish dish I was served in a Hawaiian restaurant. I liked it so much, I've cooked it many times in my own backyard. The only thing better than the sweet-and-sour-sauce is the great flavor of the fish once it's been grilled.

One 2¼- to 2½-pound whole red snapper, scaled and gutted
1 head Caramelized Garlic (page 8), pureed
¼ cup olive oil
1 onion, sliced, grilled (page 9), and chopped
1 red bell pepper, grilled (page 8) and coarsely chopped
1 small zucchini, sliced
1 small carrot, cut into thin slices
1 scallion, white part chopped, green part cut into 1-inch pieces
2 tablespoons brown sugar
2 tablespoons cider vinegar
2 plum tomatoes, grilled (page 9) and chopped
¼ cup tomato sauce (commercial or homemade)
1 tablespoon chopped fresh cilantro
½ teaspoon Tabasco
1 tablespoon cornstarch dissolved in 2 tablespoons cold water

Preheat the grill.

Rub the outside of the fish with half the garlic, drizzle with 2 tablespoons of olive oil, and grill for 4 to 5 minutes on each side, or until done.

While the fish is cooking, place a wok or flat-bottomed sauté pan on the grill or side burner. Heat the remaining olive oil, add the onion, red pepper, zucchini, carrot, and scallion, and quickly stir fry. Remove the vegetables from the pan and set aside until the fish is done.

Without washing the pan, boil the sugar and vinegar for 2 minutes. Add the tomatoes, tomato sauce, cilantro, and Tabasco. Stir the cornstarch mixture, add it to the pan, and cook until the sauce thickens, about 2 minutes. Serve the sauce over the fish.

Index

Abbachio of lamb, 47
aïoli with charred cod, 89
ale, lamb chops with, 129
Alfredo, farfalle, 35
American, veal, 74
apple(s):
  grilled, 131
  strudel, 108–109
  stuffing, 105
  stuffing, smoked duck with, 104
arugula and olive salad, 26

Barbecue(d):
  burrito, 164
  burrito rub, 165
  burrito sauce, 166
  meatballs, 43
  steamed pork buns, 206–207
barley, smoked fish, and buttermilk soup, 114
basics of grilling, 7–15
basil olive oil, 14
basil-tomato dressing, 31
bean:
  black, and onion relish, 189
  and ham soup, 140–141
  turkey-and-black-bean wontons, 211–212
beef:
  barbecued meatballs, 43
  carpetbag steak, 215
  empanadas, 167–168
  frikadeller and cheesy dill sauce, 115
  grilled Hungarian goulash, 96–97
  rouladen, 98–99
  rub, tamale, 173
  sauerbraten steak, 100–101
  shepherd's pie, 148–149
  steak pizzaiola, 44

  steak with tomatoes and olives, 45
  tamale pie, 172–173
  T-bone steak Florentine, 46
Bermudian-style pork chops, 174
bisque, hot smoked-shrimp, 70–71
black bean and onion relish, 189
black-bean-and-turkey wontons, 211–212
braciolette, veal, 48–49
bread, imam flat, 194–195
bread salad, Tuscan (panzanella), 30
breast of duck, seared, with greens and grilled fruit,
    72–73
bronzino, 60
bronzino sauce, 61
broth, tomato-mussel, grilled oysters in, 78–79
bruschetta with a trio of cheeses, 27
bubble and squeak, 144–145
buns, pork, barbecue steamed, 206–207
burgers, venison, 126
burrito, barbecue, 164
  rub, 165
  sauce, 166
buttermilk, smoked fish, and barley soup, 114

Cabbage-potato soup, 94
cacciatore, chicken, 53
Calabrese style red snapper, 62
calamari and red onion salad, 24
Canadian grilling, 123–135
caramelized garlic and tomato dip, 23
caramelized garlic olive oil, 13
caramelized new potatoes, 121
carbonara, spaghetti, 39
Caribbean, Mexican, Central and Latin American
    grilling, 159–191
Caribbean dry rub, 175
carpetbag steak, 215

carrots, glazed, 151
carrots, sherried, 152
cauliflower and grilled onion salad, 133
celery hearts, grilled, 155
Central and Latin American, Mexican, and
        Caribbean grilling, 159–191
charcoal turkey steaks, 130
charred cod with aïoli, 89
charred stuffed trout, 150
cheese(s):
    bruschetta with a trio of, 27
    chicken with smoked ham and fontina,
        56
    and eggplant fingers, 22
    macaroni and (grilled ham, cheese, and pasta),
        142–143
    potatoes au gratin, 81 .
    scaloppine of chicken fontina, 58
    and wild mushrooms, spaghetti with, 42
cheesy dill sauce, 116
cheesy dill sauce and frikadeller, 115
chicken:
    barbecue burrito, 164
    cacciatore, 53
    cock-a-leekie soup, 139
    Cuban stew, 180–181
    fontina, scaloppine of, 58
    fontina, scaloppine of, sauce, 59
    in garlic sauce, 88
    and garlic soup, 34
    grilled, smothered with mushrooms,
        102–103
    paella, 86–87
    piccata, 54
    salsa, 181
    salsa for, 182
    scarpariello, 55
    smoked, dry rub, 184
    smoked, enchiladas, 183–184
    with smoked ham and fontina, 56
    stock, 11
    sweet-and-sour, 217
    tamale, 170
    wings for the queen, 138
chili linguine, poblano, 161
chili pork chops, 177
chops, lamb, with ale, 129

chops, pork:
    Bermudian-style, 174
    chili, 177
chorizo sausage:
    Cuban stew, 180
    empanadas, 167–168
clam pie, 64–65
cock-a-leekie soup, 139
cod, charred, with aïoli, 89
cod, salt, potatoes with, 57
corn ratatouille, zucchini stuffed with,
        157
corn salad, tinned, 153
creamed spinach salad, 120–121
crostini, 28
croutons, grilled rye, 93
Cuban stew, 180–181
cucumbers, grilled, with dill, 154
curry marinade, 199
cutlets, pork, with lemon glaze, 103

Dill, grilled cucumbers with, 154
dill sauce, cheesy, 116
dill sauce, cheesy, and frikadeller, 115
dip, caramelized garlic and tomato, 23
dipping sauce, wonton, 213
dressing:
    tomato-basil, 31
    vinaigrette, 15
dry rub:
    Caribbean, 175
    smoked chicken, 184
duck:
    seared breast of, with greens and grilled fruit,
        72–73
    smoked, with apple stuffing, 104
    vinaigrette for, 73

Eggplant:
    and cheese fingers, 22
    grilled, with toasted pine nuts,
        202–203
empanadas, 167–168
enchiladas, smoked chicken,
        183–184

Index

222

Farfalle Alfredo, 35
fettuccine with scallops, shrimp, and
    radicchio, 36–37
filling, pork tamale, 171
fingers, eggplant and cheese, 22
fish:
    bronzino, 60
    charred stuffed trout, 150
    herring salad, 106
    hot smoked trout, 132
    Provençal sauce for, 76
    red snapper, Calabrese style, 62
    seafood sausage, 117–118
    smoked, barley, and buttermilk soup, 114
    stock, 12
    sweet-and-sour, 218–219
    tuna and tomatoes, Sardinian style, 63
    tuna steaks with honey-mustard marinade,
      75
    see also shellfish; specific fish
flat bread, imam, 194–195
Florentine style T-bone steak, 46
fontina:
    chicken, scaloppine of, 58
    chicken, scaloppine of, sauce, 59
    and smoked ham, chicken with, 56
French grilling, 69–82
frikadeller and cheesy dill sauce, 115
fruit, grilled, and greens, seared breast of
    duck with, 72–73
fruits, grilled, 10

Garlic:
    caramelized, and tomato dip, 23
    caramelized, olive oil, 13
    and chicken soup, 34
    and plantains, shrimp with,
      185–186
    sauce, chicken in, 88
    and vinegar, plantains with, 190
German grilling, 91–111
glaze(d):
    carrots, 151
    lemon, pork cutlets with, 103
    mushrooms, 134
goulash, grilled Hungarian, 96–97

gratin, potatoes au, 81
Greek stuffed peppers, 201
greens and grilled fruit, seared breast of
    duck with, 72–73
grill cover, 6
grilled:
    apples, 131
    celery hearts, 155
    chicken smothered with mushrooms,
      102–103
    cucumbers with dill, 154
    eggplant with toasted pine nuts, 202–203
    fruit and greens, seared breast of duck with,
      72–73
    fruits, 10
    ham, cheese, and pasta (macaroni and cheese),
      142–143
    Hungarian goulash, 96–97
    lobster spedini, 66–67
    maple-, rutabaga, 135
    meats, 10
    moussaka, 196–197
    onion and cauliflower salad, 133
    oysters in tomato-mussel broth, 78–79
    peppers and veal, 50
    pineapple and lentils, 187
    pork threads, 84
    pretzels, 110–111
    radicchio and hot pepper salad, 25
    rye croutons, 93
    tomato rice, 176
    vegetables, 8–9
    vegetarian lo mein, 214
    see also specific recipes
grilling:
    basics, 7–15
    Canadian, 123–135
    French, 69–82
    German, 91–111
    Italian, 17–68
    Mexican, Central and Latin American,
      and Caribbean, 159–191
    Middle Eastern, 193–201
    Pacific Rim, 205–219
    Scandinavian, 113–121
    Spanish, 83–89
    in United Kingdom, 137–158

Ham:
  and bean soup, 140–141
  bubble and squeak, 144–145
  celery hearts, grilled, 155
  grilled, cheese and pasta (macaroni and cheese),
    142–143
  smoked, and fontina, chicken with, 56
herb vinegar, 15
herring salad, 106
honey, Swiss chard with, 82
honey-mustard marinade, tuna steaks with,
    75
horseradish-mustard sauce, 146
hot:
  pepper and grilled radicchio salad,
    25
  pepper oil, 13
  smoked pork tenderloin, 19
  smoked-shrimp bisque, 70–71
  smoked trout, 132
Hungarian goulash, grilled, 96–97

Imam flat bread, 194–195
individual Yorkshire puddings,
    158
Irish stew, 147
Italian grilling, 17–68

Lamb:
  abbachio of, 47
  chops with ale, 129
  grilled moussaka, 196–197
  Irish stew, 147
  shepherd's pie, 148–149
  on skewers, 198
Latin and Central American, Mexican, and
    Caribbean grilling, 159–191
lemon glaze, pork cutlets with, 103
lemon olive oil, 14
lentils and grilled pineapple, 187
lentil soup, 92–93
linguine, poblano chili, 161
lobster spedini, grilled, 66–67
lo mein, grilled vegetarian, 214
Lyonnaise potatoes, 80

Macaroni and cheese (grilled ham, cheese, and
    pasta), 142–143
mac topping, 143
maple-grilled rutabaga, 135
marinade:
  curry, 199
  honey-mustard, tuna steaks with, 75
Marsala, veal, 51
meatballs, barbecued, 43
meats, grilled, 10
medallions, pork, with melon, 21
melon, pork medallions with, 21
Mexican, Central and Latin American, and
    Caribbean grilling, 159–191
Middle Eastern grilling, 193–201
minestrone, 32–33
moussaka, grilled, 196–197
mushroom(s):
  glazed, 134
  grilled chicken smothered with, 102–103
  risotto with, 40–41
  salad, 156
  wild, and cheese, spaghetti with, 42
mussel-tomato broth, grilled oysters in, 78–79
mustard-honey marinade, tuna steaks with, 75
mustard-horseradish sauce, 146

New potatoes, caramelized, 121
nuts, toasted, 10
nuts, toasted pine, grilled eggplant with,
    202–203

Olive(s)
  and arugula salad, 26
  and tomatoes, steak with, 45
olive oil:
  basil, 14
  caramelized garlic, 13
  hot pepper, 13
  lemon, 14
onion:
  and black bean relish, 189
  grilled, and cauliflower salad, 133
  red, and calamari salad, 24
  sauce, 200

oysters, grilled, in tomato-mussel broth, 78–79
oyster stew, 77

Pacific Rim grilling, 205–219
paella, 86–87
panzanella (Tuscan bread salad), 30
pasta:
    farfalle Alfredo, 35
    fettuccine with scallops, shrimp, and radicchio,
        36–37
    grilled ham and cheese (macaroni and cheese),
        142–143
    poblano chili linguine, 161
    spaghetti carbonara, 39
    spaghetti with wild mushrooms and cheese, 42
peanut sauce, 210
pepper(s):
    grilled, and veal, 50
    hot, and grilled radicchio salad, 25
    hot, oil, 13
    red, relish, 188
    stuffed, Greek, 201
piccata, chicken, 54
pie:
    clam, 64–65
    sauerkraut, 107
    shepherd's, 148–149
    tamale, 172–173
pineapple, grilled, and lentils, 187
pine nuts, toasted, grilled eggplant with, 202–203
pizza, imam flat bread, 194–195
pizzaiola, beef steak, 44
pizza toasts, 29
plantains:
    and garlic, shrimp with, 185–186
    with garlic and vinegar, 190
poblano chili linguine, 161
pork:
    barbecued meatballs, 43
    buns, barbecue steamed, 206–207
    chops, Bermudian-style, 174
    chops, chili, 177
    cutlets with lemon glaze, 103
    medallions with melon, 21
    posole, 178
    rub, posole, 179

-sausage and potato casserole, 127
skewers with rosemary, 128
smoke rub, 20
spare ribs teriyaki, 216
spice rub, 85
tamale filling, 171
tenderloin, hot smoked, 19
threads, grilled, 84
posole, 178
posole pork rub, 179
potato(es):
    -cabbage soup, 94
    au gratin, 81
    Lyonnaise, 80
    new, caramelized, 121
    and pork-sausage casserole, 127
    with salt cod, 57
poultry rub, 140
pretzels, grilled, 110–111
Provençal sauce for fish, 76
puddings, individual Yorkshire, 158

Queen, wings for the, 138

Radicchio:
    grilled, and hot pepper salad, 25
    scallops, and shrimp fettuccine, 36–37
ratatouille, corn, zucchini stuffed with, 157
red onion and calamari salad, 24
red pepper relish, 188
red snapper, Calabrese style, 62
relish:
    black bean and onion, 189
    red pepper, 188
rice, grilled tomato, 176
risotto with mushrooms, 40–41
rolls, spring vegetable, 208–209
rosemary, pork skewers with, 128
rouladen, beef, 98–99
rub:
    burrito barbecue, 165
    Caribbean dry, 175
    pork smoke, 20
    pork spice, 85
    posole pork, 179

poultry, 140
    seafood, 38
    smoked chicken dry, 184
    tamale beef, 173
rutabaga, maple-grilled, 135
rye croutons, grilled, 93

Safety tips, 5–6
salad:
    calamari and red onion, 24
    cauliflower and grilled onion, 133
    creamed spinach, 120–121
    grilled radicchio and hot pepper, 25
    herring, 106
    mushroom, 156
    olive and arugula, 26
    tinned corn, 153
    Tuscan bread (*panzanella*), 30
salsa chicken, 181
salsa for chicken, 182
salt cod with potatoes, 57
saltimbocca veal, 52
Sardinian style tuna and tomatoes, 63
sauce:
    barbecue burrito, 166
    bronzino, 61
    cheesy dill, 116
    cheesy dill, and frikadeller, 115
    garlic, chicken in, 88
    horseradish-mustard, 146
    onion, 200
    peanut, 210
    Provençal, for fish, 76
    scaloppine of chicken fontina, 59
    for seafood sausage, 119
    wonton dipping, 213
sauerbraten steak, 100–101
sauerkraut pie, 107
sausage:
    chorizo, Cuban stew, 180
    chorizo, empanadas, 167–168
    pork-, and potato casserole, 127
    seafood, 117–118
    seafood, sauce for, 119
scallops, shrimp and radicchio fettuccine, 36–37
scaloppine of chicken fontina, 58

scaloppine of chicken fontina sauce, 59
Scandinavian grilling, 113–121
scarpariello, chicken, 55
seafood:
    rub, 38
    sausage, 117–118
    sausage, sauce for, 119
    see also fish; shellfish; *specific fish*
seared breast of duck with greens and grilled fruit,
    72–73
shellfish:
    clam pie, 64–65
    grilled lobster spedini, 66–67
    grilled oysters in tomato-mussel sauce, 78–79
    hot smoked-shrimp bisque, 70–71
    oyster stew, 77
    paella, 86–87
    seafood sausage, 117–118
shepherd's pie, 148–149
sherried carrots, 152
shrimp:
    with garlic and plantains, 185–186
    scallops, and radicchio fettuccine, 36–37
    smoked-, bisque, hot, 70–71
    tamale, 170
skewers:
    lamb on, 198
    pork, with rosemary, 128
smoked:
    chicken dry rub, 184
    chicken enchiladas, 183–184
    duck with apple stuffing, 104
    fish, barley, and buttermilk soup, 114
    ham and fontina, chicken with, 56
    pork tenderloin, hot, 19
    rub, pork, 20
    -shrimp, hot, bisque, 70–71
    trout, hot, 132
    vegetable soup, 162–163
snapper, red, Calabrese style, 62
sopaipillas, 191
soup:
    chicken and garlic, 34
    cock-a-leekie, 139
    ham and bean, 140–141
    hot smoked-shrimp bisque, 70–71
    lentil, 92–93

Index

minestrone, 32–33
posole, 178
potato-cabbage, 94
smoked fish, barley, and buttermilk, 114
smoked vegetable, 162–163
spaghetti carbonara, 39
spaghetti with wild mushrooms and cheese, 42
Spanish grilling, 83–89
spare ribs, pork teriyaki, 216
spätzle, 95–96
spedini, grilled lobster, 66–67
spice rub, pork, 85
spinach salad, creamed, 120–121
spring rolls, vegetable, 208–209
steak(s):
  beef, pizzaiola, 44
  carpetbag, 215
  charcoal turkey, 130
  sauerbraten, 100–101
  tamale pie, 172–173
  T-bone, Florentine style, 46
  with tomatoes and olives, 45
  tuna, with honey-mustard marinade,
    75
  venison, 125
steamed pork buns, barbecue, 206–207
stew:
  abbachio of lamb, 47
  Cuban, 180–181
  grilled Hungarian goulash, 96–97
  Irish, 147
  oyster, 77
stock:
  chicken, 11
  fish, 12
strudel, apple, 108–109
stuffed:
  peppers, Greek, 201
  trout, charred, 150
  zucchini with corn ratatouille,
    157
stuffing, apple, 105
  smoked duck with, 104
sweet-and-sour:
  chicken, 217
  fish, 218–219
Swiss chard with honey, 82

Tamale(s), 168–169
  beef rub, 173
  chicken filling, 170
  pie, 172–173
  pork filling, 171
  shrimp filling, 170
T-bone steak Florentine style, 46
tenderloin, pork, hot smoked, 19
teriyaki, pork spare ribs, 216
tinned corn salad, 153
toasted nuts, 10
toasted pine nuts, grilled eggplant with, 202–203
toasts, pizza, 29
tomato(es):
  -basil dressing, 31
  and caramelized garlic dip, 23
  grilled, rice, 176
  -mussel broth, grilled oysters in, 78–79
  and olives, steak with, 45
  and tuna, Sardinian style, 63
topping, mac, 143
trout:
  charred stuffed, 150
  hot smoked, 132
tuna:
  steaks with honey-mustard marinade, 75
  and tomatoes, Sardinian style, 63
turkey:
  -and-black-bean wontons, 211–212
  steaks, charcoal, 130
Tuscan bread salad (panzanella), 30

United Kingdom, grilling in, 137–158

Veal:
  American, 74
  barbecued meatballs, 43
  braciolette, 48–49
  and grilled peppers, 50
  Marsala, 51
  saltimbocca, 52
vegetable(s):
  grilled, 8–9
  smoked, soup, 162–163
  spring rolls, 208–209

vegetarian lo mein, grilled, 214
venison:
  burgers, 126
  steak, 125
vinaigrette:
  dressing, 15
  for duck, 73
vinegar:
  and garlic, plantains with, 190
  herb, 15

Wild mushrooms and cheese, spaghetti with, 42
wings for the queen, 138
wonton dipping sauce, 213
wontons, turkey-and-black-bean, 211–212

Yorkshire puddings, individual, 158

Zucchini stuffed with corn ratatouille, 157